MA

AND EDUCATION

There was only one Karl Marx, but there have been a multitude of Marxisms. This concise, introductory book by internationally renowned scholar Jean Anyon centers on the ideas of Marx that have been used in education studies as a guide to theory, analysis, research, and practice. *Marx and Education* begins with a brief overview of basic Marxist ideas and terms and then traces some of the main points scholars in education have been articulating since the late 1970s. Following this trajectory, Anyon details how social class analysis has developed in research and theory, how understanding the roles of education in society is influenced by a Marxian lens, how the failures of urban school reform can be understood through the lens of political economy, and how cultural analysis has laid the foundation for critical pedagogy in U.S. classrooms. She assesses ways neo-Marxist thought can contribute to our understanding of issues that have arisen more recently and how a Marxist analysis can be important to an adequate understanding and transformation of the future of education and the economy. By exemplifying what is relevant in Marx, and replacing that which has been outdone by historical events, *Marx and Education* aims to restore the utility of Marxism as a theoretical and practical tool for educators.

Jean Anyon is Professor of Social and Educational Policy in the Urban Education Doctoral Program at the Graduate Center of the City University of New York.

Routledge Key Ideas in Education Series

Series Editors: Greg Dimitriadis and Bob Lingard
Freud and Education, Deborah P. Britzman
Marx and Education, Jean Anyon

MARX

AND EDUCATION

JEAN ANYON

Routledge
Taylor & Francis Group

NEW YORK AND LONDON

First published 2011
by Routledge
711 Third Avenue, New York, NY 10017

Simultaneously published in the UK
by Routledge
2 Park Square, Milton Park, Abingdon, Oxon OX14 4RN

Routledge is an imprint of the Taylor & Francis Group, an informa business

Typeset in Minion by Glyph International Ltd.
Printed and bound in the United States of America on acid-free paper by
Walsworth Publishing Company, Marceline, MO

Library of Congress Cataloging-in-Publication Data
Anyon, Jean.
Marx and education / Jean Anyon.
   p. cm.
1. Marx, Karl, 1818-1883–Knowledge–Education. 2. Education–Philosophy. 3. Critical
pedagogy–United States. 4. Educational sociology–United States. 5. Educational
equalization–United States. 6. Social classes–Economic aspects–United States. I. Title.
LB675.M232A69 2011
370.1–dc22   2011000309

ISBN 13: 978-0-415-80329-8 (hbk)
ISBN 13: 978-0-415-80330-4 (pbk)
ISBN 13: 978-0-203-82961-5 (ebk)

CONTENTS

SERIES EDITOR'S INTRODUCTION

This series introduces key people and topics and discusses their particular implications for the field of education. Written by the most prominent thinkers in the field, these 'key ideas' are read through the series' authors' past and present work, with particular attention given to the ways these ideas can, do, and might impact theory, research, practice, and policy in education.

More specifically, these texts offer particular conversations with prominent authors, whose work has resonated across education and related fields. Books in this series read as conversations with authorities, whose thinking has helped constitute these ideas and their role in the field of education—yesterday, today, and tomorrow.

Much more than introductions alone, these short, virtuosic volumes look to shape ongoing discussions in the field of education by putting the field's contemporary luminaries in dialogue with its foundational figures and critical topics. From new students to senior scholars, these volumes will spark the imaginations of a range of readers thinking through key ideas and education.

INTRODUCTION

Accepting a Lifetime Achievement Award from the American Educational Research Association in May, 2010, I offered the following statement:

> Thank you very much for this award. Because I have always rowed against the current of educational research, with the ideas of Karl Marx as guide and inspiration, it is especially gratifying to know my work is appreciated by this organization. But the award is not just mine; it goes to all of us in my generation and after who have written from left of center in education.
>
> The introduction of neo-Marxist ideas and concepts into education in the late 1970s and '80s gave us a vocabulary to talk about the social context of education, and the social struggles in and surrounding it.
>
> Before Bowles and Gintis published *Schooling in Capitalist America* in 1976, and Mike Apple published *Ideology and Curriculum* in 1979, most discussions of child learning were psychological—could the child 'conserve volume,' as Piaget had predicted s/he should? Educational research was positivistic and oriented toward

control—as in the Skinner stimulus-response paradigm. Most education conversations centered on technocratic, mechanistic, and behavioral aims—exemplified by Ralph Tyler's widely regarded theory of building the curriculum around a series of behavioral objectives.

Also, in the decades after the Second World War, education was typically viewed as ideologically and socially neutral—not affected by dominant hegemonic ideas, not culpable in social or economic oppression, and unrelated to political economic opportunity structures, racism, or sexism. If anything, schools were seen as 'the great equalizer,' as Horace Mann had described them in the 19th century.

With exceptions like John Dewey and George Counts, education scholarship before my generation mostly involved the study of teaching and learning isolated within schools and classrooms, unaffected by life outside; curriculum was thought of as unrelated to the needs and interests of power elites or a student's experience in school, and was thought to be largely unaffected by the student's social class, race, or the dominant ideologies of the society.

I remember my excitement upon reading Bowles and Gintis. It was 1976, and I felt trapped in cognitive psychology and psycholinguistics, writing a dissertation on the linguistic theories of Jean Piaget and Noam Chomsky.

In Bowles and Gintis' *Schooling in Capitalist America*, I saw an alternative model of educational analysis—a way to talk about education that would allow me to bring in the social: social class as important, the economic and political constraints and exclusions of capitalism as relevant to what occurred in schools, and the power of dominant ideas to shape what counted as curriculum. I finished my dissertation and began to retool myself to explore these new ideas. I joined a study group and began to read Karl Marx.

As a new professor, I engaged in research exploring the notion that schools were not neutral: they contributed to the reproduction of social classes, the economy, and racial and gender exclusion and subordination. I wanted to demonstrate ways in which the political economy was tightly bound with what happened inside school buildings.

But—as Marx had argued—struggle in the form of public contestation might also wring increased equity from the system or—as we put it then—such struggle might produce 'fundamental social transformation.'

Among those who wrote in a Marxist vein in education in the late 1970s and early '80s were Mike Apple, Henry Giroux, and myself. We agreed, as Mike Apple argued, rather than being neutral, "educational issues are at root ethical, economic, and political..." (1979,12).

The development of neo-Marxist ideas in U.S. education research and analysis was a project soon joined by others, who were also influential in the development of this work—Stanley Aronowitz, Donaldo Macedo, Cameron McCarthy, Peter McLaren, Carlos Alberto Torres, and Lois Weis, in particular. More scholars were soon writing in a radical vein as well. These colleagues include, in somewhat chronological order: Ira Shor, Rich Gibson, Bill Ayers, Martin Carnoy, Dennis Carlson, Kathleen Weiler, Kevin Vinson, Gary Anderson, Lois Weiner, Pauline Lipman, Kathleen Kesson, Antonia Darder, Rudolpho Torres, Bill Watkins, Ellen Brantlinger, Gustavo Fishman, Kathy Emery, David Gabbard, David Hursh, and most recently, Sheila Macrine, Ramin Farahmandpur, David Gabbard, Wayne Au, and Zeus Leonardo.

Of course, despite our considerable work over the years, mainstream policies still have characteristics of the old paradigms, and although federal policies like No Child Left Behind and Race to the Top contextualize education in conditions of race and poverty, they maintain much of the positivistic, behavioral goals of earlier decades. And most school reformers in U.S. cities continue to ignore the contribution of the political economy to urban school failure. But I think my generation, and those who followed, have changed the understanding of what school is and what it does in society. That is, I believe we have substantially changed the conversation. I don't think mainstream scholars, politicians, or reformers could argue with legitimacy today that education has nothing to do with the political–economic context of schools and neighborhoods. And it would be difficult to assert convincingly that race, social class, and gender do not impact learning in significant ways. School, it is now widely understood, is an institution that is not socially neutral, but tends to be strongly supportive of the goals and processes of the system and its mainstream ideas—and thus, those who profit most from these. It took the work of many scholars to change the conceptual paradigm that had been dominant. So I would say that the Lifetime Achievement Award you are giving to me is recognition of all our work, and goes to all of us on the Left who have been inspired by Marx's progressive vision.

Several months before the award, the publisher of this book asked me to produce a volume that traced the trajectory of my scholarly work over the years as an example of how Marx has been used as a guide to educational analysis. I have been pleased to carry out this request. The resulting book, *Marx and Education*, briefly explicates the ideas of Karl Marx—who emboldened us with his vision of democratically shared economic resources, goods, and profits. My main focus is on studies I have done. But in the chapters that follow, I discuss the scholarship of a few other writers as well—scholars who were important to me during that time period. I admire the many other colleagues who have been inspired by Marx, but must limit myself to including them only in footnotes, or in brief references to their work.[1]

Our research and analysis typically flowed from three basic concepts of Marx's theories: capitalism is a primary source of systemic social, economic, and educational inequality; social class is an explanatory social and educational heuristic; and an analysis of the culture that accompanies the capitalist system can be a source of neo-Marxist practice—critical classroom pedagogy. In much of this work, and in our considerable political activity on behalf of social equity in and outside of educational settings, we viewed class conflict as an engine of social change and justice.

While the late 1970s, '80s, and '90s saw a relative explosion of Marxist scholarship in education (as well as other academic disciplines), the first decade of the 21st century has experienced far less use of Marx as a guide to study or practice. As I give talks in universities around the country, I find that most young scholars and teachers, although they do understand the importance of the social context of education, are not aware of how we arrived at that assessment. Nor—if the published literatures are correct—do the vast majority in my audiences appear to avail themselves of Marx's theories in their scholarship, teacher preparation work, educational administration,

---

1 Those of us in the U.S. developing neo-Marxism in education in the late 1970s and 1980s learned a lot from our British contemporaries—scholars like Paul Willis, Michael F.D. Young, Roger Dale, Geoff Whitty, Stuart Hall, and Madeleine Arnot.

or K-12 teaching. I dedicate this book to them—researchers, administrators, and teachers who may be persuaded to take a look at Marx, and perhaps apply his vision to the deep problems we face in education at all levels. The final chapter of this book updates Marx's theory, in an attempt to bring his ideas more clearly in line with 21st century issues and problems.

Basic Ideas of Karl Marx

Karl Marx was born in 1818 in Trier, Germany. He obtained a doctoral degree in philosophy in 1841, writing his dissertation on Greek philosophy. Then he developed interest in the ideas about socialism that were swirling in newly industrializing Germany. He began to investigate the harsh working conditions in the new factories, and the poverty of the people employed there; his voluminous writings eventually made him a foremost critical analyst of the capitalist economic system.

However, while there was only one Karl Marx, there have been a multitude of Marxisms. Basic ideas expressed by Marx—for example: that capitalism is inherently contradictory and prone to crisis; that social class is central to personal exploitation, privilege, and social change; and that class struggle by the industrial working class is key to revolutionary transformation—have been ignored or reworked by others calling themselves Marxists in ways that not only contradict each other, but contradict what Marx actually said. Scholars have used Marx to argue for structuralism as well as for existentialism; to write history, and to announce the end of history; to celebrate the power of individual consciousness, and the demise of personal agency. Denigrating descriptions and uses of his ideas with which he did not agree, Marx wrote in 1882, "If anything is certain, it is that I myself am not a Marxist" (In Engels, Letter to Eduard Bernstein).

Likewise, social commentators in various countries have used Marx to foster social revolution as well as to repress it (as in the Soviet Union). Although as it has turned out, no country (with the possible exception of Cuba) has been successful in putting into practice Marx's ideas of democratically distributed economic resources and profits.

Let me briefly articulate my version of what Marx said about the basic concepts of capitalism, social class, and ideology.

Capitalism, in Marx's terms, is an economic system based on private ownership of the means of production. That is, factories, businesses, stores—corporations of all types—are not owned jointly by employees and owners, but by owners, who obtain the profits from sales. Private ownership of the means of production in capitalism is distinct from the ancient feudal system in which the means of production (i.e., the land, as the means of producing food) was held in common. Neither serf nor Lord owned the land in feudal times; each had rights and responsibilities (however unequal) regarding the common use of the land and what grew on it.

Capitalism's private ownership of production is also distinct from a socialist/communist system as imagined by Marx, in which everyone contributes to the production of economic goods according to their ability, and is provided profits and goods according to what each person needs.

An important insight of Marx was that capitalism is an economic system that can not function without fundamental inequality—meaning that inequity is built in to the way the system works. Business owners must make a profit to survive, and those who do not own businesses must find jobs and work in these enterprises, if they are to provide for themselves and their families. Workers (and other employees) are commodities, bought and sold in the market place like any other, at the lowest price. In order to make a profit, the capitalist must pay the worker less than the product s/he made can be sold for. (If the product is a service like health care or computer work, the owner of the business must take in more money than is paid to the employees, if the business is to survive.) The extra money from selling the product or providing the service is the profit that is kept by the capitalist. It is important to note that while the profit margin of small businesses is often relatively small, large corporations—and the shareholders, executives, and managers of these businesses—typically enjoy huge profits, that dwarf the wages and salaries of employees. In 2010, for example, the salaries of Chief Executive Officers of large corporations were 300 times those of typical workers. This profoundly unequal relationship between workers/ employees and owners is at the base of the system and, for Marx, is fundamental to its definition.

Since higher salaries and employee benefits would reduce the profit margin of owners, capitalists are (by definition and in most actual cases) diametrically opposed to the interests of workers—who generally desire unions, higher minimum wages, and stronger benefits. Thus the worker/owner economic relationship can be seen as a contradictory relationship. The contradictions between the main classes (working and capitalist classes) lead to tension and continual battles (strikes, slow-downs, political demonstrations) and it is by winning these class struggles that workers can be freed from the 'chains' Marx saw holding them down in factories, offices, and other capitalist enterprises. It is this class struggle which Marx saw as ultimately leading to the overthrow of capitalism and the possible development of socialism and communism—a democratic sharing of resources and profits. Marx argued that in a socialist system, "In place of the old bourgeois society, with its classes and class antagonisms, we shall have an association in which the free development of each is the condition for the free development of all" (Marx and Engels, 1848).

In capitalism, according to Marx, economic class relations strongly influence the social situation outside the work place, affecting the domestic and civic worlds in which people live. That is, Marx argued that one's job and the economic class in which that work places a person has a huge impact on many aspects of life: it centrally affects one's living conditions, the kind of school one attends, economic and social opportunities one has or is excluded from, and one's political and other ideas and views. He argued that, "The mode of production of material life conditions the social, political and intellectual life process in general. It is not the consciousness of men that determines their being, but, on the contrary, their social being that determines their consciousness" (1859).

Marx argued, in this vein, that the economic relation and social context in which the working class exists limits the worker's ability to transcend her or his social situation. For example, Marx would have argued that it is not merit by which one advances in capitalist society so much as it is because of one's social class background and the opportunities (or lack thereof) that this background affords. Men and women, Marx argued, do have some freedom and agency, but are not as free to determine their own life chances as living in a (capitalist) democracy would suggest. "Men [and women] make their own history," he said, "but they do not make it as they please; they do not make it under self-selected circumstances, but under circumstances existing already, given and transmitted from the past" (1852).

Marx considered sexism and racism to be secondary forms of subordination or oppression—secondary to the influence of social class and one's relation to private ownership (that is, whether one is an owner or a worker). He did, however, state that one can judge the fairness of a society by assessing the condition of its women. And he analyzed in much detail the contribution of race (for example, the centuries–long slave trade) to the development of capitalism in the West. But he alleged that 'in the last instance' it is people's social class that is most fundamental to their oppression, because it is the exploitation of their labor.

In addition to the exploitation inherent in the working day (in which, as noted above, the owner sells the profit of a worker's labor for more than is paid the worker), Marx described another way in which wealth is created in the capitalist system—by acquiring private rights to commonly owned land or other resources. Marx called this process 'primitive accumulation,' and used the term to describe the closing of the feudal commons during the transition from feudalism to capitalism during the Middle Ages. Friends of the English king were, during the later decades of feudalism, given private right to land that had been used in common by all. The new landowners forced the peasants off the land so they could graze their sheep and sell the wool at market. Former peasants moved to the developing cities looking for work.

Social class is another concept of Marx which neo-Marxists in education have made extensive use of. Social class is defined as a person's or group's relation to the means of production—that is, whether your relation to factories, corporations, and other businesses is one of ownership and control, or one of worker as dependent on being hired. Marx described two main classes as characterizing the capitalist system. Members of the working class, as noted above, are in an unequal and contradictory relation to the owners who hire them. Capitalists are in ownership positions, and obtain income not from labor, but from appropriating the surplus money produced by the workers. Marx saw social class as a fundamental social category, based on the way production of goods and services is organized and distributed in the economy.

Marx also described the petty (petite) bourgeoisie, who are small business owners who own some property, but not enough to have all the work done by outside employees; family members often work in the enterprise. Marx also wrote about the middle class. The middle class is in a somewhat contradictory position between worker and capitalist: middle-class managers, for example, dominate workers in a firm, but are at the same time subordinate to capital. Like wage earners, small business owners and middle-class employees of larger firms often have dual interests—typically desiring to maintain private property and property rights, but often having other interests opposed to those of the capitalist class. Owners of small businesses, for example, often oppose monopolies or oligopolies of large companies, and their ability to undersell small businesses.

Marx predicted that, as capitalism developed over the 20th century, the middle class would shrink, as successful middle-class employees joined the capitalist class, and others sank into the proletariat. Society would ultimately be characterized by two classes—a large class of poor workers, and a small group of extremely wealthy capitalists. Capitalism, he argued, will have "simplified class antagonisms. Society as a whole is more and more splitting up into two great hostile camps, into two great classes directly facing each other— bourgeoisie and proletariat" (Marx and Engels, 1848).

In addition to utilizing Marx's analyses of the capitalist system and social class, neo-Marxists have also been influenced by his view of culture. Marx understood culture in terms of ideology—how the dominant ideas of a time and place tend to arise from and legitimate the economic relations of the society. For example, in feudal society, where the English monarch had complete autonomy, the idea of 'divine right' of kings was dominant. As capitalism developed, and serfs were removed from the land and became members of a growing proletariat, they were free to work wherever they wanted; 'freedom' became a dominant idea.

Marx argued in *The German Ideology* (1845) that "the class which has the means of material production at its disposal [i.e., industrial and financial capital], has control at the same time over the means of mental production [that is, of schools, book printing, news outlets, etc.]." He would most likely argue today that in an advanced capitalist system such as our own, government, large-scale media (where a few corporations own the main media outlets) and state education systems produce ideas and truths—the ideologies—that tend to be those that legitimate and support the profit system and, thus, those who profit most from it. These ideologies are expressed and legitimated in the institutions in which we live and learn (in schools, for example, as curriculum and individual competition). It was because of the power of ideologies promulgated by those with economic power to mold a society's children and youth that Marx said that we need to "rescue education from the influence of the ruling class" (Marx and Engels, 1848).

The notion that ideologies legitimating the power of the capitalist class permeate the educational institutions of society was central to the work of another Marxist important to education scholarship by the U.S. Left during the past decades, Antonio Gramsci. This Italian revolutionary developed the concept of hegemony to describe the dominance of capitalist ideology over subordinate groups in society (Hoare and Nowell-Smith, 1971). Gramsci argued, though, that hegemony was not laid down in some final form by capitalists or their representatives, but was constantly argued over and contested by the development of counter-narratives and struggle to liberate messages in media, schools, newspapers, and other cultural products from capitalism's ideologies. People could use their nascent 'good sense,' especially when educated by critically aware teachers, to resist such dominant ideologies that (for example) capitalism is the only form of economic organization, merit and the chance of great wealth is equally spread among us, and democratic voting overcomes economic inequality. Educational sites, in Gramsci's theory, may be inherently reproductive, but can become important places for building resistance if educators are engaged with their students in efforts to critique the culture and develop anti-hegemonic counter-narratives.

Marx also recognized the importance of educational institutions as sites of developing protest against dominant culture and social organization, but was aware of the peculiar difficulty of attempts to use education as a means of working for fundamental changes in social circumstances. At a political meeting in 1869, he remarked that, "On the one hand, a change of social circumstances was required to establish a proper system of education; on the other hand, a proper system of education was required to bring about a change of social circumstances." This contradiction is one that has long plagued progressive educators who use classrooms as cites of consciousness raising and social movement building. As Marx stated at the meeting cited above regarding this contradiction, we have no choice but to 'start where we are' and use whatever means we have at hand in the struggle against exploitation and subordination.

Why Marx Now?

Although Marx wrote over a hundred years ago, and although some of his ideas are outdated, major concepts in his theory are relevant today. In the winter of 2010, during a financial crisis and continuing recession, times are hard. Official unemployment for white workers has doubled from three years ago, and black and Latino unemployment is near 30 percent. Long term unemployment (of six months or more) is at an historic high. (In March 2010, more than 46 percent of the unemployed fell into this category.) Rates of actual joblessness (people without work who have given up looking) are almost double the unemployment figures. Personal loans are difficult to acquire, home owners have been losing their homes for lack of means to pay mortgages based on interest rates that ballooned without their foreknowledge, and many people's credit cards are maxed out. State legislatures, with declined tax receipts from loss of jobs and declined personal and business income, have cut social services. Education budgets across the country are relatively far less than they were in recent years, despite the federal stimulus moneys that became available in 2009. In such difficult times, curriculum in many urban schools shrinks to the bare bones of test prep worksheets, as art, music, and sports become distant memories. Services in poor neighborhoods and districts are cut, and low-income students and their families suffer.

More and more, middle-class jobs are disappearing, and one in ten college graduates is in a minimum wage job; over a quarter of low-wage job holders have had some college education. Since 2009, more than half the students in U.S. K-12 classrooms have been eligible for free or reduced lunch. And the proportion of students who attend high poverty schools has increased by 42 percent since 2000, with almost half of black and Latino students in such schools (and five percent of whites). A 2009 study of college completion found that 91 percent of low-income students who enter a four–year college do not finish, with most citing lack of money as the reason (Bowen, Chingos, and McPherson, 2009). In these times of high joblessness, long-term unemployment, and increasing poverty, it is not difficult to see how Marx may be relevant.

But even in good times—for example, the strong economy of the mid to late 1990s—I found that a Marxian class analysis was relevant. I cited studies in 2005 demonstrating that in this period of a strong economy, almost half of full time workers made poverty *zone* wages (up to 125 percent of official poverty levels), and the middle class was hollowing out as the vast majority of new jobs were extremely low paying (with only a quarter of new jobs projected to pay above $26,000 in 2002 dollars) (see also Ornstein, 2007). Working Americans were suffering, even as the top one percent owned more of the wealth in this country than they had since 1928.

Marx had predicted the bifurcation of the population under capitalism into two classes—rich and poor. Even the thriving economy of the late 1990s seemed to have produced close to that. Marx seems prescient.

There is an additional reason that Marx is important now, and it has to do with his ideas having fallen out of favor among scholars. The enormous growth of Marxist scholarship in U.S. colleges and universities that started in the late 1960s had abated by the early 1990s. There are many reasons, including the influence of postmodernism in academia, and the de-legitimation of allegedly communist societies like the former Soviet Union and East Germany. As a consequence, Marx has been largely absent in undergraduate and graduate programs. In education (e.g., in teacher preparation, masters, and doctoral programs), radical ideas are less called on than they were. It is true that some of the basic ideas of a Marxist analysis have altered the conversations in a few fields—sociology, anthropology, geography, and education are probably the best (if only) examples. The power of the social context, and the gross inequality in our society, for example, are now taken for granted by most academics. But the fecundity these ideas would have as part of Marx's holistic vision of society and how to change it, is lost. One purpose of this book is to highlight the usefulness of Marxist theory and practice, and introduce it in education as a counterweight to mainstream talk about standards, testing, and school reform policy.

What this Book Does

Chapters One and Two of *Marx and Education* detail some of the main points I and other progressive education scholars in education have been articulating since the late 1970s.

Among scholarship I report are those demonstrating how social class analysis has developed in research and theory, how understanding the roles of education in society is influenced by a Marxian lens, how the failures of urban school reform can be understood through the lens of the political economy, and how critical cultural analysis has laid the foundation for critical pedagogy in U.S. classrooms. As I have been arguing for some time, reform of urban school districts can not be sustained—with positive economic and social consequences for graduates—without substantial expansion of economic opportunities available to the low-income high school graduate. I detail this argument here as well.

Chapter Three assesses ways neo-Marxist thought can contribute to our understanding of issues that have arisen more recently. Political economy, for example, can help us understand the limits of current federal education policy. I demonstrate ways in which U.S. education policy substitutes for economic reform. No Child Left Behind and Race to the Top are current examples.

The manner in which progressive, Left analysis adds to today's conversations is followed by Chapter Four, in which I think about how a Marxist analysis can be important to adequate understanding and transformation of the future of education and the economy. Much in Marx is outdated. The industrial proletariat, for example, has not been, and—in the U.S., at least—can not easily be expected to act as the 'vanguard of the revolution.' 'Revolution' itself appears an old fashioned concept. In my teaching and writing, I have been attempting to exemplify what is relevant in Marx, and replace that which has been outdone by historical events. An extremely important development in neo-Marxist theory is David Harvey's (2005) concept of 'accumulation by dispossession,' which I use to update Marx. Utilizing Harvey, I expand Marx's analysis to describe the social and educational consequences of the recent financial implosion and deep recession that has dispossessed so many of us of the jobs, homes, and educational services we considered our own. The application of Harvey's concept of accumulation by dispossession provides an additional tool in Marxism, one that readers can use to reclaim what may have been taken from them by large banks and wealthy hedge funds that—by all accounts—are responsible for the massive loss of jobs and income Americans have been experiencing. Harvey's concept is a theoretical and practical weapon, potentially powerful in advancing the cause of equity in our economic and educational systems.

1

NEO-MARXISM IN EDUCATION, 1970s–1980s

My generation came of age in the rebellious 1960s, and that may be one reason that as academics many of us were attracted to a theory that challenged what we had been taught about U.S. society. Rather than focusing on meritocracy, democracy, and patriotism, as our school books had taught us, we focused on what seemed to us structural inequalities—and what we saw as systematic means by which whole groups and cultures (e.g., workers, African Americans, women) were excluded from the American Dream. Radical economists Sam Bowles and Herb Gintis, in a book reviewed in the *New York Times* in 1976—*Schooling in Capitalist America*—were the first neo-Marxists to receive wide attention in education circles. The authors argued that the experiences of students, and the skills they develop in school in different social class contexts (e.g., working-class or wealthy communities), exhibited striking correspondences to the experiences and skills that would characterize their likely occupational positions later. The authors wanted to demonstrate that the major role of the education system was not primarily meritocratic, to propel individuals and groups upward as a matter of course, but was, rather, to reproduce an amenable and differentiated work force. Social class (although race and gender later proved to be also important) determined one's future economic role. The social class of one's parents and neighborhood generally determined the kind of schooling one received, and the skills and dispositions learned there predisposed you to a similarly structured economic position in the labor force. In this view, the experience of schooling was as important as, if not more important than, the content of the curriculum to the process by which schools prepare future labor force participants.

Because of this correspondence, education did not seem to be the 'social leveler' that Americans had long been taught. Rather, schools tended to reproduce the unequal labor positions that the economic system had created. Bowles and Gintis pointed out that the vast expansion of educational opportunities since World War I (and into the middle 1970s, when they were writing), had not substantially changed the highly unequal distribution of income in society. Moreover, "despite the important contribution of education to an individual's economic chances, the substantial equalization of educational attainments over the years has not led measurably to an equalization of income among individuals" (8).

As Marx had pointed out, however, institutions and systems are typically contradictory in their effects: capitalism could have both liberating as well as oppressive effects. (The closure of the feudal commons, for example, liberated peasants from their feudal bonds, but in so doing set them free to starve in the developing cities if they could not find work.) Bowles and Gintis pointed out the contradictory nature of education: while the system of schooling certainly functions primarily to legitimate and reproduce inequality, it sometimes produces critics, rebels, and radicals.

Schooling in Capitalist America was widely read and debated by education scholars. Yet Bowles and Gintis had produced little if any empirical data to document their assertions that schools in different social class contexts produce students with skills and dispositions corresponding to their probable future jobs. As a young scholar, I decided their theory was important to examine in school settings, to see if the correspondences they theorized would occur in real classrooms.

Social Class and School Work

The research I conducted in the late 1970s examined work tasks and interaction in the fifth grade in five elementary schools in contrasting social class communities—two working-class schools, a middle-class school, and two highly affluent schools.

The first three schools were in a medium-sized city district in northern New Jersey, and the final two were in a nearby New Jersey suburban district. In each of the three city schools, approximately 85 percent of the students were white. In the fourth school, 90 percent were white, and in the last school, all were white (see Anyon, 1980, 1981, 1983, 1984).

The first two schools were designated working-class schools, because the majority of the students' fathers (and approximately one-third of their mothers) were in low-paid unskilled or semiskilled occupations, with somewhat less than a third of the fathers being skilled workers. The third school was designated the middle-class school, although because of residence patterns the parents were a mixture of highly skilled, well-paid blue collar and white collar workers, as well as those with traditional middle-class occupations such as public school teachers, social workers, accountants, and middle-managers. There were also several local doctors and town merchants among the parents.

The fourth school was designated the affluent professional school, because the bulk of the students' fathers were highly-paid doctors such as cardiologists or surgeons; television or advertising executives; successful interior designers; or other affluent professionals. While there were a few families less affluent than the majority (e.g., the families of several professors at nearby universities, as well as several working-class families), there were also a few families who were more affluent.

The final school was called the executive elite school. The majority of pupils' fathers in this school were vice presidents or more advanced corporate executives in U.S.-based multinational corporations or financial firms on Wall Street. Most family money incomes of students in this school were in the top 1 percent of U.S. family income at the time.

There are obvious similarities among United States schools and classrooms. There are school and classroom rules, teachers who ask questions and attempt to exercise control, and who give work and homework. There are textbooks and tests.

All of these were found in the five schools. But I identified differences by social class in student work tasks and conceptions of knowledge. These differences did correspond to the likely future job requirements of the children in each school.

The Working-Class Schools

In the two working-class schools, work was following the steps of a procedure. The procedure was usually mechanical, involving rote behavior and very little decision making or choice on the part of the student. The teachers rarely explained why the work was being assigned, how it might connect to other assignments, or what the idea is that lies behind the procedure or gives it coherence and perhaps meaning or significance. Most of the rules regarding work were designations of what the children are to do; the rules are steps to follow. These steps are told to the children by the teachers and often written on the board. The children are usually told to copy the steps as notes. Work was often evaluated not according to whether it was right or wrong, but according to whether the children followed the right steps. The following mathematics example illustrates these points.

One of the teachers led the children through a series of steps to make a one-inch grid on their paper without telling them that they were making a one-inch grid, or that it would be used to study scale. She said, "Take your ruler. Put it across the top. Make a mark at every number. Then move your ruler down to the bottom. No, put it across the bottom. Now make a mark on top of every number. Now draw a line from. . . ." At this point a girl said that she had a faster way to do it and the teacher said, "No, you don't; you don't even know what I'm making yet. Do it this way, or it's wrong." After they had made the lines up and down and across, the teacher told them she wanted them to make a figure by connecting some dots and to measure that, using the scale of one inch equals one mile. Then they were to cut it out. She said, "Don't cut until I check it."

The fifth grade teachers observed in the working-class schools typically attempted to control classroom time and space by making decisions without consulting the children and without explaining the basis for their decisions. The teachers continually gave the children orders. Rarely if ever did they explain why the children were to do what they were told. Only three times did the investigator hear a teacher in either working-class school preface a directive with an unsarcastic "Please," or "Let's" or "Would you." Instead, the teachers gave orders, as in, "Shut up," "Shut your mouth," "Open your books," "Throw your gum away—if you want to rot your teeth, do it on your own time." Teachers made every effort to control the movement of the children, and often shouted, "Why are you out of your seat?" Often teachers' demands seemed capricious, and not part of regular school rules or routines.

A dominant theme that emerged in these two schools was student resistance. Although some amount of resistance appeared in every school in this study, in the working-class schools it was a dominant characteristic of student–teacher interaction. There was both active and passive resistance to teachers' attempts to impose the curriculum. Active sabotage sometimes took place: someone put a bug in one student's desk; boys fell out of their chairs; they misplaced books, or forgot them; they engaged in minor theft from each other; sometimes they rudely interrupted the teacher. When I asked the children during interviews why they did these things, they said, "To get the teacher mad;" "Because he don't teach us nothin';" "They give us too many punishments." When I asked them what the teachers should do, they said, "Teach us some more;" "Take us alone and help us;" "Help us learn." Sometimes they seemed pleased to see the teacher get angry, upset.

It is fairly clear that such experiences are highly similar to the type of rote, unrewarding work tasks and disciplinary control typical in working-class jobs across the board. Unskilled industrial workers, clerical personnel, retail salespersons, health care workers—these representing large percentages of jobs in the U.S.—face work tasks and control not unlike what these working-class schools seemed to be preparing their students for. And, understandably, working-class resistance is a familiar presence in such job situations.

Middle-Class School

In the middle-class school, work was getting the right answer. If one accumulated enough right answers one got a good grade. One must follow the directions in order to get the right answers, but the directions often called for some figuring, some choice, some decision making. For example, the children often had to figure out by themselves what the directions asked them to do, and how to get the answer: what do you do first, second, and perhaps third? Answers were usually to be had in books or by listening to the teacher. Answers were usually words, sentences, numbers, or facts and dates; one writes them on paper, and one should be neat. Answers must be in the right order, and one can not make them up.

For example, math involved some choice: one may do two-digit division the long way, or the short way, and there were some math problems that could be done 'in your head.' When the teacher explained how to do two-digit division, there was recognition that a cognitive process was involved; she gave several ways, and said, "I want to make sure you understand what you're doing—so you get it right;" and when they went over the homework, she asked the children to tell how they did the problem and what answer they got.

Work tasks did not usually request creativity. Serious attention was rarely given in school work to how the children develop or express their own feelings and ideas, either linguistically or in graphic form. On the occasions when creativity or self-expression was requested, it was peripheral to the main activity, or it was 'enrichment,' or 'for fun.'

The style of control of the teachers observed in this school varied from somewhat easygoing to strict, but in contrast to the working-class schools, the teachers' decisions were usually based on external rules and regulations, for example, on criteria that were known or available to the children. Thus, the teachers always honored the bells for changing classes, and they usually evaluated children's work by what was in the textbooks and answer booklets.

It was also the case that work tasks in this school involved more of a conceptual process than in the working-class schools, in that work was less a matter of facts and skills and more a matter of traditional bodies of knowledge or 'content,' and students were offered some choice in how they, for example, carried out a math problem. Knowledge was understanding and information from socially approved sources. Good grades were a possession. Information, facts, and dates could be accumulated and exchanged for good grades and college or a job. Knowledge here, however, was not usually connected to biographies or exploratory activities of the learners, and was thus divorced from processes of personal discovery (as indeed it was in the working-class schools as well). There was, however, in this school, the sense of possibility: school knowledge has real value, if one has 'enough' of it.

It is apparent that many middle-class jobs involve more decision making, conceptual judgments, and choice than working-class jobs like clerical work or retail sales. The middle-class school, by emphasizing these skills in classes, prepares students for jobs that demand those kinds of skills— jobs like public school teaching, police and fire fighters, low and mid-level management, and other middle income employees.

Affluent Professional School

In the affluent professional school, work was creative activity carried out independently. The students were continually asked to express and apply ideas and concepts. Work involved individual thought and expressiveness, expansion and illustration of ideas, and choice of appropriate method and material. The products of work in this class were often written stories, editorials and essays, or representations of ideas in mural, graph, or craft form. The products of work should not be like everybody else's, and should show individuality. They should exhibit good design, and (this is important), they must also fit empirical reality. The relatively few rules to be followed regarding work were usually criteria for, or limits on, individual activity. One's product was usually evaluated for the quality of its expression and for the appropriateness of its conception to the task. In many cases one's own satisfaction with the product was an important criterion for its evaluation. When right answers were called for, as in commercial materials like SRA (Science Research Associates) and math, it was important that the children decided on an answer as a result of thinking about the idea involved in what they were being asked to do. Teacher's hints were often to "think about it some more."

The following activity is illustrative. Each child and his or her family had made a geoboard. The teacher asked the class to get their geoboards from the side cabinet, to take a handful of rubber bands, and then to listen to what she would like them to do. She said, "I would like you to design a figure and then find the perimeter and area. When you have it, check with your neighbor. After you're done, please transfer it to graph paper and tomorrow I'll ask you to make up a question about it for someone. When you hand it in, please let me know whose it is, and who verified it. Then I have something else for you to do that's really fun. (pause) Find the average number of chocolate chips in three cookies. I'll give you three cookies, and you'll have to eat your way through, I'm afraid!" They worked sitting or standing up at their desks, at benches in the back, or on the floor. A child handed the teacher his paper and she commented, "I'm not accepting this paper. Do a better design." To another child she said, "That's fantastic! But you'll never find the area. Why don't you draw a figure inside [the big one] and subtract to get the area?"

The teachers often used negotiation to control the class. I rarely heard them yell or scream; they attempted to reason with the children and control them through a process of give and take.

Work tasks in the affluent professional school involved not only conceptual work, but discovery, construction, and meaning making. Individuals were to express themselves in their work.

Jobs in which one is likely to be considered an 'affluent professional' include advanced computer designers, high-level positions in advertising, the arts, media; medical doctors, highly paid professors, and other positions in which creativity and use of symbol systems are manipulated and well rewarded. Control is by negotiation with one's peers and those to whom one reports. The children in this affluent professional school were receiving good preparation for that kind of work.

Executive Elite School

In the executive elite school, work was developing one's analytical intellectual powers. Children were continually asked to reason through a problem, and to produce intellectual products that were both logically sound and of top academic quality. A primary goal of thought was to conceptualize rules by which elements may fit together in systems, and then to apply these rules in solving a problem. School work helps one to achieve, to excel, to prepare for life.

The following is illustrative. The math teacher taught area and perimeter by having the children derive formulae for each. First she helped them, through discussion at the board, to arrive at $A = L \times W$ as a formula (not the formula) for area.

After discussing several, she said, "Can anyone make up a formula for perimeter? Can you figure that out yourselves? (pause) Knowing what we know, can we think of a formula?" She worked out three children's suggestions at the board, saying to two, "Yes, that's a good one," and then asked the class if they can think of any more. No one volunteered. To prod them, she said, "If you use rules and good reasoning, you get many ways. Chris, can you think up a formula?"

She later told the investigator that her goals in math are to develop their reasoning and mathematical thinking and that, unfortunately, "There's no time for manipulables [like geoboards]."

While right answers were important in math in the executive elite school, they are not 'given' by the book or by the teacher, but may be challenged by the children. Going over some problems in late September the teacher said, "Raise your hand if you do not agree." By Thanksgiving, the children did not often speak in terms of right and wrong math problems, but of whether they agreed with the answer that had been given.

The executive elite school was the only school where bells did not control the periods of time. The fifth grade teachers were very strict about changing classes on schedule, however, as specific plans for each session had been made. The teachers attempted to keep tight control over the children during lessons, and the children were sometimes flippant, boisterous, and occasionally rude. However, the children could be brought into line by reminding them that "It is up to you." "You must control yourself." "You are responsible for your work." "You must set your own priorities." One teacher told a child, "You are the only driver of your car—and only you can regulate your speed." While strict attention to the lesson at hand was required, the teachers made relatively little attempt to regulate the movement of the children at other times. For example, except for the kindergartners, the children in this school did not have to wait for the bell to ring in the morning; they could go to their classroom when they arrived at school. Fifth graders often came early to read, to finish work, or to catch up. After the first two months of school the fifth grade teachers did not line the children up to change classes or to go to gym, etc., but, when the children were ready and quiet, they were told they could go—sometimes without the teacher.

During class they did not have to sign out or ask permission to leave the room; they just got up and left. Because of the pressure to get work done, however, they did not leave the room very often. The teachers were very polite to the children, and the investigator heard no sarcasm, no nasty remarks, and few direct orders. The teachers never called the children "honey," or "dear," but always called them by name. The teachers were expected to be available before school, after school, and for part of their lunch time to provide extra help if needed.

The work tasks of the children in this school seemed to speak less to creativity or thinking independently or making 'sense' than did the work tasks experienced by the affluent professional children. Rather, the children's work in this school was academic, intellectual, and rigorous. There was an attempt to teach more, and more difficult, concepts than in any other school. Success resulted not from personal activity or attempts to make sense, but from following rules of good thought, from rationality and reasoning. In many cases, work involved understanding the internal structure of things: the logic by which systems of numbers, words, or ideas are arranged and may be rearranged. And the type of control for which the children were being prepared involved being treated with respect, as equals. They were expected to set their own priorities, internalize control, and exercise it appropriately.

Executive elite jobs are indeed those in which one is responsible for one's own self control, has control over others, and has responsibility for the system as a whole. Examples of such positions are extremely well-paid top executives in corporations, elected or appointed officials with top positions in government, and leaders of large organizations or institutions.

My research study of five schools provided empirical confirmation of Bowles and Gintis' theory of the correspondence between traits and skills learned in the education system and the needs of the economy (the labor market). The scholarly publications issuing from this research struck a cord with readers, and have been (and are being) reprinted many times. They have appeared in over 40 books edited by others. The inequities documented by the study continue to seem relevant to readers' educational experiences.

There was other important scholarly work underway in the late 1970s and '80s, however.

Capitalism and Culture

Michael Apple had been writing for several years about the ways in which culture and ideology were important to the analysis of education in U.S. society. His book, *Ideology and Curriculum*, published in 1979, laid out the first explicit and widely read neo-Marxist analysis of the relations among

U.S. culture and the economic and educational systems. Apple supported his arguments with insights from a powerful tradition of scholarship already active in Europe. He introduced many American educators for the first time to the writings of Pierre Bourdieu, Antonio Gramsci, Raymond Williams, Paul Willis, Michael F. D. Young, Geoff Whitty, and other European scholars who had been assessing the dominant cultures in their own countries and the influence of those cultures on individuals and social systems.

A neo-Marxist analysis of capitalist culture demonstrates that not only does the experience of schooling have reproductive qualities, but so does the content of learning—the formal curriculum itself.

Apple described Bourdieu's concept of cultural 'capital,' for example, explaining how the language patterns, ways of knowing, and specific bodies of knowledge of dominant groups are what the U.S. educational system validates as legitimate and therefore correct. Bourdieu had demonstrated how in France, the validation of dominant culture and cultural forms in education contributes to the reproduction of social and economic elites and of the capitalist system itself (1973). In this view, rather than intellectual ability or merit, it is access to cultural capital in the home that is rewarded by good grades in school and success in education.

Apple also introduced us to Raymond Williams' notion of a 'selective tradition,' in order to demonstrate that curriculum is not neutral in regard to knowledge, class, race, or power (for example) but reflects a process of selection. This selection, from "within the forms of an effective dominant culture, is always passed off as 'the tradition,' the significant past" (in Apple, 1979, 6). Williams argued that the selectivity is the important point, the way in which out of a universe of possible ways of seeing and acting in the world, certain meanings and practices from the dominant culture (typically, the culture of elites) "are chosen for emphasis," while "certain other meanings and practices are neglected and excluded" (ibid.). Thus in school, the knowledge and ways of seeing the world of dominant white (male) elites in U.S. society are validated by being included in the school curriculum, and students study the lives of presidents and generals, but not of the working class, blacks, or women.

And Apple brought to our attention the ideas of Antonio Gramsci. The dominant culture, in Gramsci's view, represents the interests of those in power, and is hegemonic—it is the socially legitimated view, expressed by education and other institutions such as the media. But, as Apple pointed out, ideologies that are hegemonic are not imposed by the ruling class once and for all. They are combated; counter-hegemonic views can be and are developed in the struggle for social change and justice. However, uncontested, as hegemonic culture typically is in educational institutions, the ideology saturates students and teachers alike. As Apple put it, "institutions of cultural preservation and distribution like schools create and recreate forms of consciousness that enable social control to be maintained without the necessity of dominant groups having to resort to overt mechanisms of domination" (3). We are 'incorporated' into the dominant culture in school, and develop a 'false consciousness' (7).

Apple strongly urged us to challenge curricular and organizational forms in education that legitimate and reproduce hegemony. His challenge was an important step in the development of critical pedagogy by U.S. educational scholars working in a neo-Marxist tradition. These scholars would, over the next two decades, build a well theorized body of knowledge concerning critical teaching for student empowerment. Their work typically utilized Gramsci and the notion of hegemony, but also pulled ideas put forth by other Marxist scholars such as Louis Althusser, the Frankfurt School (Theodor Adorno and Jürgen Habermas), British cultural studies (Stuart Hall, Paul Willis), and Brazilian revolutionary Paulo Freire.

Resistance

A central tenet of critical pedagogy is that students are not always incorporated into the dominant ideology; they sometimes resist. Indeed, they may resist more than we know.

Major neo-Marxist theorization of the concept of resistance was accomplished in Henry Giroux's *Theory and Resistance in Education*, published in 1983.

Giroux wanted to take us "beyond theories of social and cultural reproduction" (98) into an understanding of how student resistance to dominant cultural forms can challenge hegemony. He argued that student resistance is not merely anti-authoritarian behavior. Taking his cue from British cultural studies, he argued that resistance can take the form of youth subcultures that are challenges to the hegemonic culture. Unlike the other major scholar writing about resistance during the 1970s and early 1980s, British scholar Paul Willis, Giroux did not believe that resistance by students to school culture damages them by alienating them from the compliance that allows them to earn educational credentials. He argued for a complex notion of resistance, one that goes beyond merely oppositional behavior into a yearning for social transformation. He argued that to be adequate, a construct of resistance

> celebrates a dialectical notion of human agency that rightly portrays domination as neither a static process nor one that is never complete. Concomitantly, the oppressed are not viewed as being simply passive in the face of domination. The notion of resistance points to the need to understand more thoroughly the complex ways in which people mediate between their own lived experiences and structures of domination and constraint. ... Inherent in a radical notion of resistance is an expressed hope, an element of transcendence, for radical transformation.
>
> (108)

This politically informed call for resistance was followed in Giroux's book by a discussion of the power of critical pedagogy and the possibilities inherent in teaching students to see through the ideologies that saturate their schooling.

In this 1983 book, Giroux also made the point—as did several others at the time—that neo-Marxists ignored race and gender in their attempt to describe the power of social class to yield educational and social oppression and exclusion.

This first period of sustained writing from a neo-Marxist perspective in education—the late 1970s to 1989—established for readers that U.S. schools were not neutral in regard to social oppression or exclusion, but were crucially implicated in the reproduction of economic inequalities and social ideologies. The next period, 1990–2005, attended to the criticism that race and gender were missing from our analysis, and took neo-Marxism in new directions. My own work, for example, moved from analysis of social class manifestations in schooling to investigation of ways in which the economic and political decisions of powerful corporations and legislative bodies fundamentally shape school systems and the opportunities they present (or deny) various groups of students.

2

NEO-MARXISM IN EDUCATION, 1990–2005

Chapter One highlighted several neo-Marxist authors active in education in the late 1970s and 1980s. These efforts were an early foray into the ideological thicket surrounding U.S. schools. (Other well-known progressive voices in education during the 1980s were Stanley Aronowitz, Donaldo Macedo, Ira Shor, and Peter McLaren.) All of us challenged the dominant idea that education in this country was a-political and not involved in reproducing systemic inequalities of the economic and social systems.

In the next period, 1990 to 2005, neo-Marxist theorizing and politically progressive critical pedagogy came of age as Latino, black, and feminist scholars inspired by Marx added to analyses that centered on social class. These authors considered the consequences of race, gender, and students' culture to their school experience and economic future. In addition to the inclusion of race, gender, and culture in neo-Marxist studies, an analytical stance toward education called (radical) political economy developed, primarily in my own work (but with important research published by Pauline Lipman in 2003).

This chapter offers a brief look at the joining of race, class, feminism and culture, and then presents a somewhat detailed discussion of the contribution of radical political economy to the neo-Marxist literature.

Race, Class, Gender, and Culture

Latino writers on the Left in the 1990s challenged the traditional Marxist paradigm because it focused primarily on social class and economic exploitation. This new scholarship gave a poignant reminder that race and culture can also be causes of oppression. The authors demonstrated that Latino language, culture, and working-class status often combined to marginalize non-English speaking students. Inspired particularly by Brazilian Marxist Paulo Freire, scholars such as Carlos Torres, Antonia Darder, Gustavo Fischman, and Rudolfo Torres demonstrated how the power of Anglo culture often reaches down into classrooms to strip working-class (and other) minority students of their language and cultural beliefs. The authors argued that critical pedagogy in democratically run classrooms could empower Latino and other non-English speaking students to reclaim their cultural and social identities. Carlos Torres (1995), for example, made the case that Bowles and Gintis' correspondence/ reproduction paradigm over determined students' future status, and robbed them of agency.

Torres argued for the study of race, class and gender together, and developed a British-inspired cultural studies approach to critical pedagogy. Antonia Darder, in *Culture and Power in the Classroom* (1991), made important linkages between culture, critical theory, and democracy. She demonstrated ways that culturally rich, democratically run classrooms could provide a solid foundation for what she called 'bicultural'—beyond bilingual—education.[1]

There were also important educational analyses of the interaction of black oppression and social class, particularly by Cameron McCarthy (1999), Pauline Lipman (1998), and Bill Watkins (2001). McCarthy chastised radical scholars for research on curriculum that, he argued, treated race and racial cultures as epiphenomena of the political economy. He studied racial discourses in the media and education, and the ways these disadvantaged black students of both working- and middle-class status.

Studying the connections between race and class, Pauline Lipman argued (1998) that urban school reforms would not be successful for working-class minority students until teachers were helped to understand racial cultures and interactions in their classrooms. In 2001, Bill Watkins investigated the historical and ideological foundations of black education in the U.S., situating this history in the context of increasing industrial–corporate power around the turn of the 20th century.

---

1 I would be remiss if I did not mention the contributions of Ira Shor and Peter McLaren to neo-Marxist scholarship on critical pedagogy during these years. See Shor 1992, *Empowering Education*; and McLaren 2000, *Che Guevara, Paulo Friere, and the Pedagogy of Revolution*.

Many black educational scholars at the time found inspiration in Critical Race Theory (CRT) and the analysis and promotion of culturally relevant curriculum, rather than Marxism. CRT based its analysis on racial, rather than class, oppression. And most feminists preferred a gender lens to the Marxist one. But several progressive feminists described the ways class and gender interacted not only in the labor market (where working-class and many other women were underpaid and typically excluded from executive positions), but in the classroom (where culture, curriculum, pedagogy, and school organization can be oppressive to female students) (see Weis 1990, Fine 1991, and Weiler 1994). What might be called a 'neo-Marxist feminist pedagogy' emerged in the writings of Kathleen Weiler (1994), who brought the various strands of feminism into conversation with Freire's radical educational methods of assisting workers and Brazilian peasants to understand how the economy exploited them.

So far in this chapter I have provided examples of neo-Marxist scholarship between 1990 and 2005 that brought culture, race, and gender into radical educational discussions, challenging the traditional Marxist paradigm by going beyond the argument that the reproduction of a compliant labor force is the primary role of education systems in capitalist economies.

In a moment I will present details of a strand of neo-Marxism that focused not on culture but on the political–economic analysis of social and educational policy—my own work over the same period. But first I want to consider scholarship that provided a Left oriented cultural analysis not of race and gender, but of political and economic power. In 2001 Michael Apple published *Educating the 'Right' Way*. This book continued the economically informed analyses of dominant U.S. culture the author had undertaken throughout the 1990s—e.g., *Official Knowledge: Democratic Education in a Conservative Age* (1993) and *Education and Cultural Politics* (1996). In these two earlier books, Apple explored the resurgence of conservative forces in the U.S., describing (among other developments) the increasing influence of corporate power on education. In the last of the series, *Educating the 'Right' Way*, he argued that political, economic, social, and cultural groups on the Right had formed what Gramsci had called a 'hegemonic alliance'—a dominant cohering of powerful forces in a society. A major goal of this alliance was (and is) to move education policy toward conservative ends. Guided by a 'free market' profit-making model of education (cutting corporate taxes and installing privately funded, profit-making alternatives to public education, particularly charter schools) has been a primary aim of this conservative alliance.

In *Educating the 'Right' Way*, Apple appreciated the successful methods the Right has utilized to mold public opinion—funding and operating 'think tanks' (that produce articles and briefs supporting conservative goals), placing frequent articles and letters in major newspapers, placing spokespersons on TV and radio talk shows, and focusing in politics on 'family' culture values to deemphasize job losses and stagnant incomes caused by recurring recessions in the U.S. economy since the late 1970s.

Apple argued in *Educating the 'Right' Way* that in order to combat conservatives, progressive groups should take note of the strategies they employ, and learn from them. He urged, in this vein, that we ought to build counter-hegemonic alliances and (for example) develop counter-narratives that we place in the popular media. The coalitions Apple recommended would include working-class groups like unions, but also anti-racism organizations, anti-globalization groups, peace activists, environmentalists, feminists, and lesbian and gay groups.

Political Economy

One of the issues that motivated the 'conservative restoration' that Apple described taking place during the 1990s was an intense desire by major corporations to improve the economic competitiveness of U.S. business—which had been declining since the late 1970s, when less expensive, technologically superior cars, televisions, and other products built in Japan and Korea began flooding the U.S. market. The U.S. Chamber of Commerce and other business groups argued that the failure of the U.S. education system had been a main reason for the economic decline of American firms during these decades. Their argument was that if workers had better cognitive and technical skills, business would be more competitive. The federal government-sponsored report, Nation at Risk, famously expressed this view in 1983:

> Our Nation is at risk. Our once unchallenged preeminence in commerce, industry, science, and technological innovation is being overtaken by competitors throughout the world. This report is concerned with only one of the many causes and dimensions of the problem, but it is the one that undergirds American prosperity, security, and civility. We report to the American people that while we can take justifiable pride in what our schools and colleges have historically accomplished and contributed to the United States and the

well-being of its people, the educational foundations of our society are presently being eroded by a rising tide of mediocrity that threatens our very future as a Nation and a people.

(www2.ed.gov/pubs/NatAtRisk)

This report stimulated corporate elites and their legislative allies to an intense effort at raising education standards and testing students with state wide measures—in the hope that this would improve cognitive and technological skills of the workforce and therefore boost the economy. As Kathy Emery (2002, 2007) describes in great detail, by 1989 the Business Roundtable, a coalition of representatives from 42 of the largest corporations, had developed and promulgated among legislatures in all states and national conservative groups the criteria that would ultimately appear in George Bush's No Child Left Behind legislation, passed in 2001. A particularly intense focus on urban school reform was part of this effort.

The next chapter of this book will argue in some detail that expecting education reform to fix the problems of the economy is quite a conservative response to economic problems. For now, let me say merely that blaming the schools for economic decline is like assuming that, for example, the decline of Detroit's car economy was caused by the poor educational achievement of Detroit students. This is a patently untenable position. The collapse of the competitiveness of U.S. car makers in Detroit was a result, of course, of many factors, none of them educational: a failure by management in the 1950s and '60s to upgrade factories that had been built in the 1920s and '30s; better and cheaper products being built by Japanese and Korean firms that overtook American car sales in the 1970s; the skyrocketing cost of fuel— which made large

American 'muscle cars' more expensive to run than more fuel-efficient Japanese cars; removal of jobs from Detroit to the U. S. South, Mexico, and other countries, etc.

In any event, during the 1990s an intense effort to upgrade education, especially in the nation's large urban districts, where achievement was quite low, ensued. In this effort to improve urban schools federal, state, and local districts in cities across the country funded tens of thousands of projects like the following: establishing new math and science curricula; raising academic standards; using statewide standardized tests to measure achievement; reducing class size; improving teachers' skill; reorganizing administrative structures to include parent and teacher representatives; establishing small schools; regulating student behavior with 'zero tolerance' mandates; aligning district and state education policies governing urban districts; and increasing urban school funding.

During the national focus on urban school reform, I was on the teacher preparation faculty at Rutgers University in Newark, NJ. The district asked me to carry out one of the many school reform projects underway in the city. I would prepare teachers in one of the schools to use cooperative learning methods in their teaching.

Several years later, as a result of my experience in this school and extensive research on the city, I published *Ghetto Schooling: A Political Economy of Urban Educational Reform* (1997). Let me relate a bit of my experience at 'Marcy' Elementary School, and describe how it led me to undertake a historical study that resulted in a profound challenge to the ability of education reform to systemically upgrade urban schools.

In the mid-1990s (as in 2010), Newark—like most large U.S. cities and metropolitan areas—had many poor families and neighborhoods of concentrated poverty. Most of the schools were high poverty schools, and 78 percent of the students in the district were of low enough income to qualify for low or reduced lunch. Eighty-five percent were black or Latino. The school I worked in also had a sizeable group of homeless students, many of whom were living with relatives, or with their families who had been placed in a nearby motel.

Field notes from an early visit to a classroom at Marcy Elementary give a feel for this school:

> As I enter the room there is a strong smell of urine. The windows are closed, and there is a board over the glass pane in the door. The teacher yells at a child from her desk, "I'm going to get rid of you!" Some children are copying spelling words from the board. Several of them jump up and down out of their seats. Most are not doing the work; many are leaning back in their chairs, chatting or fussing.
>
> The children notice my arrival and look at me expectantly; I greet them and turn to the teacher, commenting on the broken pane of glass in the door. She comes over from her desk and says, "Jonathan put his hand through the window yesterday—his father passed him on the street and wouldn't say hello. Jonathan used to live with him, but since he started living with his mother, the father ignores him."
>
> "These kids have hard lives, don't they," I say. At that, she begins a litany of the troubles of the children in her class: Derrick's father died of AIDS last week; one uncle has already died of AIDS and another is sick. One girl's father took her money for drugs. On Monday a boy had been brought to school by his mother, who said that the boy had been raped by a male cousin on Thursday. The teacher was trying

to get the boy some counseling. Two boys were caught shaving chalk and "snorting the dust," and "they aren't getting any counseling either." One boy had a puffy eye because his mother got drunk after she got laid off, and beat up the kids while they were sleeping; last night he had hit her back, while she was sleeping.

At this point I interrupt the teacher to say, "It's really stuffy in here. Why don't you open a window?" "I can't," she replies, "because I have some children (points to a tiny girl) who like to jump out of school windows." The children are totally out of control now, running around the room. One boy is weeping quietly at his desk. She shouts, "Fold your hands!" They ignore her. I realize I must leave so she can get them back in some order, so I say I will see her next week, and go out the door. It locks behind me.

I visited Marcy School often, getting to know the teachers and administrative staff and hear their stories. I was soon horrified by, and very angry at, what I came to know and observe: chaos in the halls and bored children in many classrooms, punitive, stingy treatment of teachers by the district and principal, and behavior by many teachers, both black and white, toward children that (I felt) belittled and otherwise disrespected them. As a result of all this, there seemed to be very little teaching or learning going on. Field notes from my first cooperative learning workshop at Marcy school included the following:

We sat in the library, its wooden shelves built 131 years ago, and began to discuss cooperative classroom techniques. Despite the noise in the halls, fire alarms being set off by the children, the intercom blaring, and students running outside the library door, the teachers seemed attentive and involved. What they liked, they said, was that we took time to acknowledge the reality of what one called "The situation we have here!" Most workshops, they alleged, are "useless" because "They never get to the discipline part. They say they'll come back to that, but they never do." "The workshop presenters say, 'Here it is—go do it.' But we can't! There's too much going on here." The teachers said that they were referring to the extreme poverty of the children; drug use of the parents; and violence—for example, recent experiences with a gun in the school, where third graders were "shaking down" younger children for money; ongoing tumult caused by caustic relations with the principal, and what teachers felt were excessive demands of the numerous district reforms.

When I arrived two weeks later for the fourth day of workshops, the air in the school smelled acrid and foul. There had been a fire in the basement woodshop five days before. The fire had spread because the fire department, used to false alarms from the building, had not responded at first. My field notes from that afternoon's workshop read:

I couldn't focus the teachers. They were preoccupied and anxious. There was a tension in the air that you could cut with a knife. When I expressed this to Susan, an eighth grade teacher, she grimaced and said, "Yes, I feel it too." Twelve of the 25 classroom teachers (48 percent) were out, which is not unusual for a Monday, but five of the subs did not show up and did not call to say they weren't coming.

The noise in the hall was overwhelming, with kids running, shouting, and doors slamming. Where we sat around a table with the doors closed we had trouble hearing each other. The intercom, which you could not turn off, was blaring, "Teachers—lock your

> doors! They're supposed to be locked! [to keep unauthorized chil-
> dren and adults from entering the rooms]."
>   I attempted to start the workshop. It was already a half-hour late.
> I was going to use a video, but I could not get the VCR to work; a
> teacher said that it had broken late last week. I felt immobilized by
> the chaos in the school.

I was prompted by these and similar experiences in teachers' classrooms in the coming weeks and months to ask myself
how things had come to such a low point. Newark schools
had, after all, been the pride of the state, and extolled in professional educational journals in the early 20th century. What
had happened? To answer this question I did not look for
explanations in African American or ethnic white (e.g., Jewish
or Italian) culture, as did many white and black inhabitants of
the city; and I did not think individuals or groups on the scene
at the time could be solely responsible for a situation that
seemed impossible to negotiate humanely. I looked to history.
I delved into a study of the city's past—concentrating on
economics and politics. I ultimately concluded that conditions in the city and in its education system were intimately
connected, and that one couldn't be fixed without fixing the
other. As I wrote then, "attempting to fix an inner city school
without fixing the neighborhood it is in is like trying to clean
the air on one side of a screen door."

I eventually arrived at four historical developments that
I believed went a long way toward accounting for the decline
in schools in Newark that had been of such renown a hundred
years ago.

1 The social class and racial status of the overall city and
   neighborhood population was closely correlated with

the level of the city's investment in education and with the district's success in educating its student population. Thus, when Newark was a leading industrial city in the early 20th century, and many children of the middle and more affluent classes attended the schools, the system was a model for others in the state. As children of different cultural backgrounds who were poor—Eastern European Catholics, Jews, and then Italians—began to predominate in the public school population, the district was unable to adequately serve significant percentages of these students. Then, beginning in the 1930s, as economic and other social changes were creating a school system in which most students were white working-class, investment and quality in all but the middle-class neighborhoods declined. After World War II, as the city schools filled with rural black poor, spending and educational quality in most city schools plummeted. By 1961, when the Newark schools were majority black poor, relative funding of the education system reached its lowest point. Continued ghettoization of the city's minority population—and educational inadequacy since then—has prevented further generations of Newark students from acquiring a worthwhile education.

2 The contours and fortunes of Newark's schools in the 20th century were also intimately linked to economic transformations of the city—and to federal and state policy as well as to local and national corporate decision making. Numerous policies and decisions contributed to the economic decimation of Newark, as the middle-class population and jobs were supported in their move to the suburbs and beyond. Among these policies are the

following: the federal redlining of city mortgage and home renovation applications beginning in the 1930s, and continuing until almost all of Newark was redlined; federal tax regulations making corporate dispersal to outside the cities cheaper than renovation in city locations; property tax laws that penalized the cities with shrinking amounts of property to tax; and decisions by local industry, banks, and insurance companies whose investment in Newark was for most of the century limited to the downtown business district. The transition to a service and sophisticated information base also contributed to the decimation of community jobs and city resources as corporations continued to leave Newark. As the city's economy changed and declined, the quality of the city's schools declined apace.

3 The political isolation of cities (both before and after political reapportionment in the 1960s and '70s) allowed more than a century of tax and other policies that penalized cities—and therefore their schools. Starting in the Colonial period, New Jersey, like other states, devised political mechanisms that concentrated power in rural wealthy families, at the expense later of the more populous cities. The 'One Man, One Vote' laws of the 1960s and '70s revised voting procedures so that most cities had greater representation in their states. But the suburbs soon dominated the voting ranks, and the cities' percentage of a state's vote declined again. This isolation from formal political power contributed to the sharp declines in funding of city schools nation-wide over the 20th century. The funding policies of city schools have, since the 1970s, been challenged in most states by

advocates of poor school districts. The resulting positive decisions and resulting reform efforts, however, have to date been too little and too late to reverse over a century of neglect.

4 In part because of the absence of sufficient economic resources and entry level jobs (for example) and political under-representation in state and federal legislatures, for most of the last 100 years the city schools have been enmeshed in local networks of corruption and patronage run by white ethnic (Jews, then Italians)—and more recently African American—minorities. Over a century of political appointments in the schools of Newark contributed to a staff that was over the years less qualified than that in surrounding suburban districts.

I argued in the book that these historical trends in Newark, this historical political economy, resulted in the educational system requiring reform that goes far beyond new science and math curricula, smaller classes, higher standards, and standardized testing. The crucial reason these reforms are not sufficient is that they fail to reach into the neighborhoods and overcome many decades of urban economic decline and the race and class ghettoization of the population.

I concluded that in order to reverse the decline of schools in cities like Newark, we needed to revitalize the cities and their neighborhoods, and make the reform of schools part of a broader strategy for social change. This broader strategy would be one in which educational reformers would join with community development and government sponsored organizations that could create jobs, train city residents for entry level as well as more sophisticated positions, offer legal services, build low and mixed income housing and health clinics and hospitals, and register voters. To be fully effective in upgrading education, such coalitions would need to be accompanied by educational reforms like full funding of urban districts through higher taxes on corporations and other wealth, renewal of administration and teaching through productive staff development, etc. (Anyon, 1997; see also Anyon 1994, 1995a, and 1995b).

It was through the process of working in Marcy school and researching the city's corporate, governmental, and neighborhood history that I developed the radical political economy I have utilized since then. I would follow *Ghetto Schooling* a few years later with a book I called *Radical Possibilities*, which brought the political economy into conversation with 21st century social policy.

Ghetto Schooling was quite successful for an academic book. Reviewed in the *New York Times* and many other publications, it has sold to date over 26,000 copies (a typical academic book sells fewer than 1,000 copies). The arguments I made stimulated lots of discussion at conferences and in journals. As a result of my analysis (and work by other progressive scholars like Pauline Lipman [1998, 2003] and Pedro Noguera [2003]) policy makers and school reformers have been made aware of the limited potential of reform policies aimed only at schools, isolated from the social context. Unfortunately, however, like much academic work, while *Ghetto Schooling* may have strongly affected the educational conversation, it seems to have had minimal if any influence on actual school reform policy or practice in U.S. cities. For instance, President Obama's Race to the Top is based on the acknowledged difficulty that poverty adds to the problem of educating urban poor students well, yet none of the reforms encouraged by this national policy actually attempt to reduce that poverty—say, by creating neighborhood jobs through which parents might improve their income and access to other resources.

A graduate student once told me that the course of history in *Ghetto Schooling* seems "unrelenting." She said, "The past seems to be an unrelenting march toward disaster in Newark and its educational system." Indeed, it does. In my research and analysis, I had concentrated on the corporate and governmental policies and practices that had brought the city to its knees. I did this because it had not been done before, and needed doing. I felt that if we were really going to make a systemic, sustainable difference in urban schools, the power of past economic and political decisions to trump school reforms that ignored the consequences of these decisions had to be demonstrated. But in my desire to catalogue the injustices perpetrated on cities like Newark, I had neglected the many actions of residents over the years to fight back.

As I contemplated my next research project, I thought about my own life experience. I had been born into a politically progressive family, and had participated in two social movements—the 1960s Civil Rights Movement, and the movement to end the war in Vietnam. I resolved to bring a focus on people contesting injustice into my scholarship.

I published *Radical Possibilities: Public Policy, Urban Education, and a New Social Movement,* in 2005 (see also Anyon, 2006). The first part of the book documents social policies that deeply affect urban education because they serve to maintain concentrated poverty in American cities. I describe some of these policies below. The second part of *Radical*

Possibilities lays out principles and strategies by which educators can work—and work together with others—to change these policies. I offer a brief recounting of this advice to close the chapter.

The most obvious federal policy that maintains poverty for working people is minimum wage legislation. Congress set the first minimum wage in 1938 at $3.05 (in 2000 dollars). In 2005, before it was raised slightly in 2007, it stood at $5.35—a mere two dollars more. Yearly income at this wage is $10,712. In July, 2009, the federal minimum wage increased to $7.25, the third and final step in a minimum wage increase Congress authorized two years earlier. With this last increase, many of America's lowest paid workers received a raise; but this still leaves the real value of the minimum wage lower than it was 30 years ago (Filion, 2009).

Minimum wage standards directly affect the wages of almost nine percent of the workforce; and when we include those making one dollar more an hour than the minimum wage, this legislation affects the wages of as much as 19 percent of the workforce—almost one in five. And because most workers of color are in low-wage employment, a disproportionate percentage of people in minimum wage jobs are black or Latino.

There are other macroeconomic policies whose consequences produce hardship. These also especially burden the lives of blacks and Latinos. Among such policies are job training as a predominant federal anti-poverty policy when there have been too few jobs for graduates of these programs; ineffective federal implementation of policies that outlaw racial discrimination in hiring and housing; regressive income taxes that charge wealthy individuals less than half the rate charged during most of the first 60 years of the 20th century, when rates on the top dollars of wealth were between 70 and 91 percent. Yet current tax policies substantially raise the payroll taxes paid by the working poor and middle class; and corporate tax policies in recent years allow 60 percent of the largest U.S. corporations to pay no federal taxes at all (and in some cases to obtain millions in rebates) (see Anyon, 2005 for documentation).

The effects of these policies are compounded by harsh union laws and lack of federal protection for labor organizing; Federal Reserve Bank pronouncements that ignore the portion of its mandate to maintain a high level of employment; federal trade agreements that send thousands of corporations—and their job opportunities—to other countries; and more.

Also important in maintaining poverty are policies that would help but are conspicuous by their absence: for example, regulation of the minimum wage that kept low-paid workers' income at the median of highly-paid, unionized workers in the decades after World War II; federal programs for urban youth that would support college completion; a program of job creation in cities; and policies to enforce laws against discrimination in hiring.

Social scientists concerned about poverty have investigated the unequal distributions of public and private investment, production, labor, and housing that characterize the typical U.S. metropolitan area—a city and its surrounding suburbs. Research has found the following: most entry level jobs for which low-income urban adults are qualified are located in the outlying suburbs; federal and state public transportation systems do not connect these job centers to areas where low-income minorities live, thus preventing poor people from commuting to jobs there; state allowed local zoning on the basis of income prevents affordable housing in most suburbs where entry level jobs are located; failure to enforce antiracial housing discrimination statutes confines most blacks and Latinos to poor city neighborhoods and segregated suburbs, where jobs are few; and federal and state taxes paid by residents throughout metro regions (including inner cities) support development that takes place primarily in the affluent suburbs. These inequitable regional arrangements contribute in important ways to joblessness and poverty in cities and inner ring, urbanized suburbs, and to the poor quality of services such as public education there.

Contemplating these policies, knowing that only 11 percent of low-income students who graduate from high school have the funds to complete college or other post-secondary degrees, and aware of the likelihood of their future unemployment or minimum wage positions, I thought, "How can even a successfully reformed urban school benefit a low-income student of color whose graduation will not lead to a job on which to make a living because there are not enough such jobs, and will not lead to the resources for college completion?" New curriculum, standardized tests, or even nurturing democratic small schools do not create living wage jobs, and do not provide poor students with the funds and supports for a bachelor's degree, which could make a significant difference in their lives. It seemed to me that we must change these political/economic policies. But how?

Social Movements and Teaching

To answer this question, I drew on the vision of political struggle that was part of Marx's theory. I knew political struggle has the potential and sometimes the power to challenge (and replace) laws that are harmful to working people, blacks and Latinos, and women (among other groups). In 2003 I began a study of the history of political activism in the U.S., and found that most, if not all, of the laws and policies that have increased equity for under-served groups have been wrought by decades of concerted political contestation—in other words, by social movements.

For example, over a century of active political struggle was necessary to obtain the most fundamental voting and other civil rights for black Americans. Five decades of labor battles were necessary before legislation in 1938 finally provided an eight hour day, a 40 hour work week, a minimum wage, and the legal end to child labor. This decades-long, vociferous advocacy also culminated in the 1930s in the right to overtime pay, unemployment insurance, social security, and the freedom to organize unions. Previously, over 20 years of activism were required before white women were permitted to vote in 1920.

And social movements have changed education. The radical tumult of the early 20th century Progressive Era opened public schools to the community in many cities, and increased educational opportunities for working-class immigrant families in the form of kindergarten, vacation schools, night school, social settlement programs, and libraries. As a result of the Civil Rights Movement Head Start, a radical innovation by activists in Jackson Mississippi, moved to center stage in federal educational policy; and segregation of blacks in public schools became illegal. Because of the high segregation of U.S. metro areas, the South, in a 2001 study, was found to be the only region of the country where whites typically attended schools with significant numbers of blacks. In the 1970s and

'80s, the women's, disabilities, and bilingual education movements also had significant impacts on schooling—opening up opportunities previously denied great numbers of students. And lastly, in recent years, a movement of an invigorated political Right has pushed both America and its schools in conservative directions. Education, economic opportunities, and civil rights have all been weakened by the rise of an organized, well funded politically conservative movement.

But there are also a number of small social movements on the Left today—state-wide, metro area, and a few national coalitions fighting against the policies I describe in *Radical Possibilities* and for power in urban communities. I portray in depth some of these groups and campaigns in the book, and argue that we need to form coalitions between and among them, in the hope of building a national movement for economic and educational justice.

The last chapter of *Radical Possibilities* places educators at the center of attempts to build a politically progressive social movement. Urban teachers who are respectful, caring, hardworking educators, trusted by students and parents, have a unique opportunity to engage students and their families in political activity—and are in a good position to join with neighborhood activist groups already in motion.

Among the strategies I suggest teachers and administrators use to make schools and classrooms into social movement building spaces are the following:

1 In order to mobilize students and families politically, a culture of trust and support must be created in the school. One small step in developing trust is to immerse classrooms in narratives that counter the dominant

media and scholarly stories of failure and deficits of students of color. Theresa Perry, in 2004, provided ideas teachers can use to counter the damaging social 'truths' about minority students. Her methods build an "intentional classroom community spirit" of education for "racial freedom, uplift, citizenship and leadership" (93). In a school culture where students and families are valued and respected, it is very possible for a teacher or principal to engage families in activities that challenge school districts and governments to make meaningful changes in neighborhoods and schools.

2   Part of developing this positive culture could include inviting parents and other caretakers into schools as change agents, rather than as volunteers. For example, an angry parent can be viewed as an opportunity, instead of a threat. An angry parent presents an opportunity to organize families to, for example, demand increased accountability of officials and politicians. If one parent is angry, others may be also, and that anger can be turned to constructive uses by teachers and administrators.

3   All large cities, and many small ones, have politically active groups working for school reform, affordable housing, and better jobs (for descriptions of some of these organizations, see *Radical Possibilities*). Invite members of local activist groups into the classroom as resources for student projects. Include in lesson and unit plans requirements that students interview members of activist groups to obtain their opinions and viewpoints. The suggestions below build on connections between educators and communities, including local activist organizations.

4   Every community has assets that can be utilized to improve life for residents. Classroom maps can be made of where these assets are located in neighborhoods of the city. Such assets include skills of residents of all ages; churches and religious leaders; tenant associations and community development corporations; parks, businesses, and hospitals; and local or statewide organizations of Democrats, Republicans, and progressives (like the Green Party), among others. Community assets can be mapped to show places of opportunity (health care, education), markets (jobs), and city structures such as transportation. On the map should also be noted areas in the community where these assets are needed (see http://www.communityyouthmapping.org).

5   Asset mapping should be used as the basis for carrying out a 'power analysis.' Such an inquiry assesses the causes and solutions of current problems, whether these extend from the neighborhood and city to the state or federal levels. A power analysis identifies a problem faced by students and other community residents and asks questions such as, Who is impacted by the problem? Who makes decisions that determine community outcomes? What kinds of informal influence or formal power do community residents have over the situation? Who are potential allies in an attempt to solve the problem? When specific names and addresses are added to an asset map in answer to these questions, it becomes a power map.

6   A power map can be used to develop an issue campaign with students. As *Radical Possibilities* explains in great detail, teachers and students can build a campaign

identifying a problem and possible solutions and share their plan of potential action with residents of the community, district leadership, corporate representatives, and government officials. In general, an issue campaign begins when students identify a problem of concern, then identify and map local needs, resources, and visions for change. They can conduct surveys and interviews, delve into city archives and newspaper stories, and collect demographic and geographic data. The class analyzes what they have found out about the problem and possible solutions, making power maps of who holds power to fix what is wrong. Importantly, the teacher contacts community groups working on the same or similar issues for support and ideas. The students decide how they will disseminate their research and solutions—with posters, letters, news and TV releases, even demonstrations. In all likelihood, they will not create waves of change; but they will learn that they are capable of working for social change (and are not merely social 'problems' as the media and education systems typically view them).

In this chapter I have argued that historical and recent political economic practices create issues for urban neighborhoods and schools that no existing educational policy or urban school reform can transcend. In this view, low-achieving urban schools are not primarily a consequence of failed education policy, or urban family dynamics, as mainstream analysts and public policies typically imply. Failing public schools in cities are, rather, a logical consequence of the U.S. macroeconomy—and the federal and regional policies and practices that support it. Teachers, principals, and urban students are not the culprits—as reform policies that target increasing testing, educator quality, and the control of youth assume. Rather, an unjust economy and the policies through which it is maintained create barriers to educational success that no teacher or principal practice, no standardized test, and no 'zero tolerance' policy can surmount. It is for this reason that I argued in *Radical Possibilities* that macroeconomic mandates continually trump urban educational policy and school reform.

I want to turn now to other issues that concern us. Congress has legislated two major education policies that every U.S. district and school are expected to respond to. These policies, of course, are No Child Left Behind, and Race to the Top. I have serious reservations about the assumptions underlying these mandates, and in the next chapter I articulate this critique.

3

CURRENT ISSUES: ECONOMIC PROBLEMS, EDUCATION POLICIES

In 2005, the final year of the previous chapter's story of neo-Marxist educational scholarship, the world seemed to most Leftists and liberals a nasty place. By 2005, conservative hard-liners were in charge, former President George Bush had invaded a country on false pretenses of 'weapons of mass destruction,' and we were paying for, and fighting but not winning, two separate wars. Democrats and Republicans alike had slashed the social safety net for low-income families until it was the weakest of any advanced capitalist country in the world. A very small group of families and individuals had captured almost a quarter of the wealth in the United States. Education and teachers were being pushed and pulled so that students were tested, tested, tested, with scant progress to show for it.[1] As the consequences of standardized testing increased, more and more urban low-income students dropped out of school (or, according to some, were 'pushed out' to increase test performance of their schools). I, for one, felt that things couldn't get much worse.

But a financial crisis of staggering proportions hit the globe in December, 2007, and continues still as severe recession in the U.S., with jobs hard to find and long-term unemployment at an historic high.

Financial crises and recessions have rattled the U.S. economy repeatedly since the early 1980s, when Ronald Reagan's government began the dismantling of a regulatory structure that—since its inception during the Great Depression—had successfully prevented banks and other large investors from taking financial risks that could disrupt or crash the U.S. economy. The regulatory legislation created by Franklin Delano Roosevelt's administrations helped the U.S. economy survive the Great Depression; and between the end of World War II and Ronald Reagan's first term (the coming to power of neoliberal, market based policies) there had been no severe recession in the U.S.

We have been in a different economic period since the early 1980s. Frequent severe economic crises, and diminished education in the service of state exams is our reality. Several brutally frank CEOs of major banks, as well as most pundits on the Left, have argued that the financial regulation bill passed in summer 2010 has little capacity to place but minor bumps in the road that large banks and investors have been traveling.

---

1 After achieving some gains in student test scores in the early part of the decade, the nation's schools have seen progress stall since 2007.

As I noted in the Introduction, many millions in the U.S. are unemployed, and millions more are underemployed, and making poverty wages.

How can a Marxist analysis contribute to our understanding of what has occurred and is facing us? Does a radical viewpoint provide a useful lens on what should be done to provide financial health to America's 140 million strong work force? And how does education fit into the picture? This chapter attempts to answer these questions, by providing some clarity on what needs to be done to provide low and middle income families with good jobs and decent income.

Economic Issues, Education Reform

Barak Obama, who campaigned on a platform of liberal-sounding change, has adopted an approach to the jobs crisis that is remarkably similar to that of conservative former President George Bush. That is, both regimes have counted on education to solve the problems of unemployment and increases in poverty.

This chapter argues that Race to the Top, and its antecedent No Child Left Behind, are policy substitutes for economic reform—reforms like the creation of good jobs for low and middle income workers, including the requirement that employers pay decent wages, provide health care, and pensions.

Employers big and small would find these requirements onerous, as such legislation would decrease the decision-making freedom and the profits of business. Moreover, economic reforms like these are often (wrongly) labeled 'socialism' by conservatives, to forestall their enactment.

Neither Democratic nor Republican administrations seem willing to fight for economic reforms that would substantially benefit low and middle income employees. Instead, education reform replaces needed economic change.

But massive job creation for the unemployed by the federal government was accomplished successfully in the 1930s, and continued in some form until Ronald Reagan eliminated it. Such jobs typically used public money, not private corporate funds. Economists state that public job programs are relatively inexpensive. And by providing income to people who did not have it, the jobs are a strong stimulus to the U.S. economy, where 60 percent of economic activity is by consumers. Examples of jobs that need to be done, for people who need work, include "labor-intensive service jobs in fields like education, public health and safety, urban infrastructure maintenance, youth programs, elder care, conservation, arts and letters, and scientific research" (Shiller, 8/1/10).

In the Introduction, I mentioned that corporate and political elites often argue that education must be reformed because it is a prime determinant of U.S. economic competitiveness. While there is merit to the argument that education contributes to U.S. competitiveness, the main determinants of economic competitiveness are economic, not educational. I offered the case of Detroit as an example. In this chapter, I focus on a different assumption underlying NCLB and Race to the Top. This second assumption motivating the educational policies is that more education will get a person a good job and thereby reduce poverty and inequality.

For example, former president George Bush stated that "The No Child Left Behind Act is really a jobs act, when you think about it" (Third Presidential Debate. Oct. 13, 2004).

And the 2010 White House fact sheet for Race to the Top states that, "The reforms contained in the Race to the Top will help prepare America's students to graduate ready for college and career, and enable them to out-compete any worker, anywhere in the world" (http://www.whitehouse.gov/the-press-office/fact-sheet-race-top).

One assumption underlying these statements—that more education will get people jobs and therefore raise their standard of living and decrease poverty and inequality—sounds plausible enough, given the fact that those with a college degree earn more than most who have only a high school degree. However, there are serious fallacies in the federal assumption, and I believe these fallacies are fatal to the utility of education as a replacement for the actual creation of economic opportunities.

The first fallacy of the premise is that for several decades now, more education and skills—that is, higher productivity—has no longer been rewarded with higher pay. American workers are more productive than they have ever been, primarily because they have more education and technological skills; but wages and salaries for most have declined. The late 1990s was the only period of broad-based gains for American low and middle income workers since the early 1970s.

American families typically lose ground during a recession. The first decade of the 21st century was not the first time that middle and low-income families lost ground in a recession, nor was it the first time that their losses continued after a recession ended. But before a business cycle ends—before the next recession starts—real median incomes usually start to grow and ultimately surpass their prior high. Yet, according to labor economists at the Economic Policy Institute, in this first decade of the 2000s, the longest jobless recovery on record damaged families' earnings capacity, and increased inequality; moreover the growth that did occur by-passed low and middle income families, going to the top few of the highest earners, leading to dramatic increases in inequality (Mishel, Bernstein, and Shierholz, 2009).

The sharp rise of income inequality has contributed to the disconnection between productivity and broadly shared income gains. The most comprehensive data on inequality demonstrates an historic rise in inequality. Data on income concentration going back to 1913 shows that "The top 1% now holds 23% of total income, the highest inequality level in any year on record, but one: 1928. In the last few years alone, $400 billion of pretax income flowed from the bottom 95% to the top 5%, a loss of $3,660 per household in the bottom 95%" (ibid.,3). (Changes to the tax system under former President Bush have exacerbated the problem by lowering tax rates of those at the top of the income scale much more than those in the middle, or at the low end.) U.S. low and middle income job holders are relatively highly skilled; and they work more hours than in other advanced capitalist countries; but they are not being given the proceeds of their increased productivity.

The second fallacy in the assumption underlying NCLB and Race to the Top (that increased education and skill will be rewarded by better jobs and higher pay for most students) is that there are in fact very few jobs that pay well or that demand high cognitive and technological skills. The jobs the U.S. economy has been producing for the last few decades are primarily poverty and low-wage jobs (low-wage being income slightly above the poverty level). The economy creates relatively few highly paid positions—making it increasingly less certain that more education will assure that work pays well.

In 2005 I cited studies demonstrating that 77 percent of new and projected jobs in the next decade will be low-paying. Only a quarter of these were expected to pay over $26,000 a year (in 2002 dollars). More recent research confirms that trend, and concludes that from 2000 to 2006, the share of good jobs in the economy actually dropped—such that in 2006 only 23.1 percent of jobs paid at least $17 per hour and offered both health and pension benefits (the definition of a 'good job'). This drop in the number of good jobs occurred during a period when the workforce was becoming both older and more educated on average, which according to federal policy assumptions should have increased the number of good jobs and pay.

Even college graduates have seen entry level wages falling. Between 2000 and 2007, female college graduates' entry level wages fell 1.7 percent and those of males fell 3.2 percent. In fact, the only period of rising wages for entry level male college graduates since 1973 was 1995–2000 (ibid., 171).

Even though more education does not guarantee a good job any more, it is certainly true that a college degree typically increases the lifetime earnings of an individual over someone with just a high school diploma. Unfortunately, very few low-income students continue on to the baccalaureate. A 2009 study found that 68 percent of affluent students but just nine percent of students from low-income families receive a bachelor's degree, and only ten percent of students entering community college eventually obtain a college degree (Bowen, Chingos, and McPherson, 2009). A 2010 assessment of reasons for non-completion found that the vast majority of the low-income students who do not finish cited prohibitive college costs as a main reason for non-completion

(Advisory Committee on Student Financial Assistance, 2010). An education policy that would certainly be useful here is full funding of low-income high school graduates who are admitted to college. I return to this recommendation later.

It remains true, however, that even for individuals who do graduate from college, success in today's economy is not assured. One reason for this is that a college degree is required for only a small percentage of new jobs. In 2005, I wrote that of the 20 occupations expected to grow the fastest, only six require college degrees—these are in computer systems and computer information technology fields, and there are relatively few of these jobs overall. (Many other of the fastest growing positions require on-the-job training.) A 2009 report by the US Department of Labor makes similar predictions concerning the relatively low levels of education that will be needed by the vast majority of working people: in 2006, the occupational demands of jobs required that only 27.7 percent of the workforce have a college degree or more. The Department of Labor predicts this share will rise by one percentage point to 28.7 percent by 2016 (Mishel, Bernstein, and Shierholz, 2009).

Even before the recession that took hold in 2008, a college degree did not guarantee a decent job. In 2005, one of six college graduates was in a job paying less than the average salary of high school graduates. Between 8.8 percent and 11 percent of people with a bachelor's degree made around the minimum wage. This means that an increasing number of college graduates—about one in ten—was employed at poverty wages. Even the education levels of welfare recipients are higher than ever. The share of welfare recipients who had high school degrees increased from 42 percent in 1979 to more than two-thirds (70 percent) in 2008 (ibid.). Welfare recipients are more educated, but still poor.

There are other reasons that more education may not increase one's chances of a better job and higher pay. Gender discrimination, for example, can work to reverse—or even eliminate—wage gains that accrue to individuals with more education. Female high school graduates earn less than male high school dropouts. During the 2000s, women with post-bachelor's degrees earned less than men who had just a bachelor's. If you are female, more education does not necessarily mean higher wages.

Race as well can cut into the benefits of further education. A study of entry level workers in California discovered that black and Latino youth had improved significantly on every measure of skill in absolute terms and relative to white workers. Yet their wages were falling further behind those of whites. In this example, the deleterious effects of racism outweighed the benefits of education, with minority workers at every level of education losing ground to similarly-prepared whites.

Various other economic developments—such as lack of unionization, multiple free trade agreements that outsource jobs, and increasing use of part-time workers—cut across the college–wage benefit, lowering it significantly for large numbers of people, most of whom are minorities and women.

Because of these economic realities, even if all low-income students tested well in school and graduated from high school and then college, only a few would obtain high-paying jobs demanding high cognitive and/or technical skills, because there are not enough of these jobs to go around. There are not now, nor have there been for more than two decades, nearly enough jobs for those who need them. Labor economist Gordon Lafer demonstrated that over the period 1984 to 1996—at the height of an alleged labor shortage—the number of people in need of work exceeded the total number of job openings by an average of five to one. In 1996, for example, the country would have needed 14.4 million jobs in order for all low-income people to work their way out of poverty. However, there were at most 2.4 million job openings available to meet this need; of these, only one million were in full-time, non-managerial positions (2002). And with the recession maintaining high unemployment in 2010, the situation is far worse.

A final problem I want to mention that circumscribes the utility of Race to the Top's emphasis on 'education for jobs' is that when low-income students and students of color do graduate from college, it is almost always from a public institution, rather than a more selective or private institution. Affluent white students, on the other hand, typically attend and graduate from more selective schools (Carnevale and Strohl, 2010). This stratification of college attendance by social class matters, because for one thing, selective institutions spend up to $92,000 per student, while colleges with low selectivity spend about $12,000 per student. And per-pupil subsidies at selective universities are eight times greater than at non-selective institutions. Moreover, the prestige and networks one acquires at a selective school are invaluable in future job searches. Given these fallacies in the argument that higher education standards and more difficult tests will pull people out of poverty by allowing them to obtain good jobs, it would make sense to actually create good jobs for people who need them. Realistic anti-poverty policy would have to include the creation across the board of good jobs for the unemployed and those living in poverty. If we expect more than a few low-income students who achieve at high levels to obtain better jobs, we need to begin creating those jobs.

Realistic anti-poverty policy would also include significant raises in the minimum wage. Indeed, during the three decades following World War II, when working-class Americans prospered, the minimum wage was indexed to the wages of well-paid, unionized, industrial workers: when their wages increased, so did the wages of the un-unionized.

I want to state clearly: education did not create the problem of wide-spread poverty and low-wage work, and education will not solve the problem. Race to the Top will not raise wages for the millions who work at poverty jobs. Only employers and governments can raise wages. The situation demands, it seems to me, real job creation—in addition to better and more education.

Race to the Top and NCLB privatize a number of central education functions—instruction (private tutoring) and organization (charters) being only two examples. The laws encourage and support huge increases in private company provision of school services like student transportation and food, test development and preparation, data analysis and management, staff development, remedial services, and content area-specific programming (Burch, 2009). The policies are often criticized for the ways in which they attempt to privatize a publicly owned function by moving to a capitalistic market model in which educational service creates profits for private business. Schools that fail to raise test scores, for example, give way ultimately to vouchers or charters in the market model, but first to a variety of expensive, pre-packaged curricula, testing, and tutoring programs. As a result, companies by 2005 had already accrued billions of dollars in profit (Bracey, 2005). Among the largest beneficiaries of No Child Left Behind were long-term business friends of President George Bush—e.g., the McGraw family of test-makers CBT-McGraw Hill, powerful lobbyist Sandy Kress, and the developers and publishers of Reading First, a billion-dollar-a-year, federally funded primary reading program for which districts must compete (ibid.). Large beneficiaries of Race to the Top, which mandates the development of charter schools as one of four reforms, will be charter school operators. The privatization built into NCLB and Race to the Top accelerates the 20th century trend toward shaping public education in the interests of corporate concerns. My concluding argument in this chapter builds on this point.

The Social Costs of Poverty

I have alleged that NCLB and Race to the Top are federal legislative substitutes for policies that would actually lower poverty and inequality—legislation that would create jobs with decent wages and benefits for those who do not have them. My critique has been that an assumption underlying these policies, that increased educational achievement will ultimately reduce poverty, does not prove valid for large segments of the population. I want to make a further point here.

If businesses were mandated by law to create jobs for those who need them—and if businesses had to pay decent wages and benefits—the costs to business owners would be enormous. As we know, neither small nor large corporations pay such costs now. Instead, the costs of the poverty produced by insufficient and poorly-paid employment are passed on to the tax-paying public in the form of programs to compensate: public tax dollars pay for welfare, food stamps, the costs of incarceration, and Medicaid—among other publicly-funded programs that attempt to ameliorate the individual and social pain of unemployment and underemployment (see Anyon and Greene, 2007).

When the federal government and the business communities rely on education to reduce poverty, the social costs of the failure of such an approach are enormous, and taxpayers shoulder the burden.

Radical political economists have pointed out that in the last half century taxpayers have paid for an increasing number of supports that make private business—especially large corporate conglomerates—profitable. Economist James O'Connor noted in 1973 that taxpayers have increasingly paid for more infrastructure, research and development, and education for business needs:

> Capitalist production has become more… dependent on science and technology, [with] labor functions more specialized, and the division of labor more extensive. Consequently, the monopoly sector [energy conglomerates, concentrated banking and finance, giant information technology firms, and manufacturing]… requires increasing numbers of technical and administrative workers. It also requires increasing amounts of infrastructure (physical overhead capital)—transportation, communication, R&D, education, and other facilities. In short, the monopoly sector requires more and more social investment in relation to private capital…. The costs of social investment… are not borne by monopoly capital but rather are socialized and fall on the state [i.e., upon tax payers].

(24)

That is, public funds subsidize the research and development, technology, infrastructure and education that the corporate community says it needs.[2]

I want to extend O'Connor's argument to include the social costs of the poverty produced when jobs are lacking and pay is low. When businesses and large corporations pay poverty or low wages to 41 percent of the people working full-time in America, as I demonstrated in *Radical Possibilities*, the costs of supporting people's needs are socialized to the tax-paying public, just as the technological and other costs of doing business have been. The private sector is not liable for the social costs of the poverty its actions produce.

NCLB and Race to the Top are part of this process of socializing the costs of poverty. When the Acts assume—even implicitly—that poverty is a result of low scores on standardized tests, rather than a result of the fact that there are not enough decently paying jobs, it lets the business community off the hook. It saddles the poor with unrealistic expectations and the rest of us with unwitting support of corporate irresponsibility.

Instead of the federal attempt to use standardized testing, merit pay, and charter schools (all required by Race to the Top) to fight poverty, I would suggest (in addition to the creation of good jobs) two education policies that might provide

---

2 At the same time that tax moneys supporting corporate needs have increased, corporate contributions to local and national taxes have decreased significantly. In 1957, corporations provided 45 percent of local property tax revenues in the states, but by 2002, the corporate share of total state and local taxes paid was 2.9 percent. The share of the federal tax burden paid by corporations declined from 40 percent in the 1940s, to 26.5 percent in 1950, to 9.2 percent in 2001 (Anyon 2005).

traction in assisting low-income students in their efforts to climb the socioeconomic ladder.

First, as I have already mentioned, the U.S. should fully fund and otherwise support all low-income students who are accepted by a college or university. *Rewarding Strivers*, edited by Richard Kahlenberg (2010), provides details on ways some universities are already assisting low-income students. These schools could be models for federal support. In addition, there is a historical precedent for funding the post-secondary education of those who cannot pay. After the Second World War, the federal government funded the education and support of over 8 million returning soldiers and their families. I see little reason we could not do the same for our college going low-income youth today.

The second education policy I recommend flies in the face of the 'college for all' mandate so prominent today. A low-income student who graduates from high school and is not able to complete the college degree has few if any economic options. We might begin to think about providing meaningful vocational options for these students while they are still in high school. Ideally, this policy would accompany the creation in urban areas of good jobs where the graduates of high school vocational programs would be hired. In New York City, for example, where I live, there is an extreme shortage of skilled auto mechanics. High schools in the area with large numbers of low-income students could offer up to date instruction in this subject for their non-college going youth, and pair the students with local high end employers. These policies are complementary: fully fund those students who get into college so they can finish; and provide real vocational preparation for those who do not attend college.

This chapter has taken issue with two of the most influential federal education policies of our time. As a radical political economist, I have concentrated on systemic inequalities; I have tried to point out ways in which macro structures like legislated national policy are affected by (and may affect) the economy. As an educator, I attempted to link these regularities to education and to assess the consequences of this connection. So far, neo-Marxist thought has served me well. But there are future issues that Marx's theory is not well equipped to assess. The last chapter attempts an extension of Marxist theory that may prove useful in both our theorizing and political practice.

4

EXTENDING MARXIST THEORY AND PRACTICE

Referring to current concerns that a neo-Marxist analysis might illuminate, I made the point in the last chapter that we are in the midst of an economic era that had its beginnings in the 'Reagan Revolution' of the early 1980s. Since that time the U.S. has developed record-breaking inequality, a financialized economy that crashed and burned and left millions of people unemployed and some homeless (as their mortgage payments rose out of reach and their homes were repossessed), and federal education policy that purports to deal with the economic crises of inequality and poverty but cannot. This chapter explores a different aspect of inequality than Chapter Three, which discussed economic (jobs and income) inequalities and attempts by the government to reduce these through education policy. The present chapter views inequality through the lens of recent fundamental changes in the economy. These changes have to do with the financialization of our system of profit making. The U.S. economy used to create profit for business owners and shareholders almost solely by providing products and services to the U.S. (and other) consumers. Now, however, the economy functions less and less to produce products and services for consumption, and more and more to create profits for a small elite of wealthy bankers and other investors through complex financial speculation. A major consequence of economic financialization is the astounding increases in inequality in our country that I have been referencing throughout this book (see Lipman, in press, for global consequences of financialization).

I want to make the point now about inequality that this radically increased unequal distribution of income has serious consequences not just for the poor and unemployed, but for all of us. Former U.S. Secretary of Labor Robert Reich explains:

> In 1928 the richest 1 percent of Americans received 23.9 percent of the nation's total income. After that, the share going to the richest 1 percent steadily declined. New Deal reforms, followed by World War II, the GI Bill and the [1960s] Great Society expanded the circle of prosperity. By the late 1970s the top 1 percent raked in only 8 to 9 percent of America's total annual income. But after that, inequality began to widen again, and income reconcentrated at the top. By 2007 the richest 1 percent were back to where they were in 1928—with 23.5 percent of the total. Each of America's two biggest economic crashes occurred in the year immediately following these twin peaks—in 1929 and 2008. This is no mere coincidence. When most of the gains from economic growth go to a small sliver of Americans

at the top, the rest don't have enough purchasing power to buy what the economy is capable of producing. America's median wage, adjusted for inflation, has barely budged for decades.

(in press)

Reich makes the fundamental argument that extreme inequality was the underlying cause of both the Great Depression and the 2008 Great Recession. That is, extreme inequality of income is unsustainable; it undermines consumer capacity (which, as I have pointed out, provides 60 percent of the economic activity in this country). Inability of the public to purchase goods and services induces economic recession as demand falls, more employees are laid off or let go, and consumer activity shrinks further. (What is not mentioned in this excerpt from Reich's book is that most of the largest corporations are not dependent on U.S. consumers for sales and profits, and may continue to make money in other countries and through financial investments when sales in the U.S. falter.)

This final chapter responds to the problem of unsustainable income imbalance in the U.S. economy—and its educational consequences—by proposing two changes in the Marxist paradigm. The intent of these alterations is to render Marx's ideas of greater utility (see Anyon, 2009, for the uses of theory). Marxist theory is based on industrial capitalism as it existed in the late 19th century. Although its applicability has been demonstrated throughout this book, Marx's conceptual apparatus needs to be updated to take better account of changes in the economy such as financialization. I modernize neo-Marxist thinking by applying what I take to be the most important extension of his theory since Antonio Gramsci made us aware of the political power of culture—David

Harvey's theoretical identification of the process that he calls "accumulation by dispossession" (2005).

The second change I propose is to Marxist practice. While scholars like myself hope to raise readers' awareness of structural issues in capitalist political economy and culture through our writing, perhaps the most practical application of neo-Marxism in education has been critical pedagogy in our classrooms. As described in Chapter Two, the hope of our teaching has been to raise political consciousness in students through thought-provoking classroom activity—engaging with issues of ways black, Latino, Asian, female, native, immigrant, and gay and lesbian students can be oppressed or excluded by the educational, political, economic, and cultural systems. We encourage students to read, discuss, and write about these issues, leading, we hope, to their increased understanding of ways the capitalist system oppresses or excludes them. As progressives, we also hope that students will carry over classroom teachings and insights into their life outside schools.

However, in my experience, and in reports from educators in high schools and colleges elsewhere, these classroom activities may lead to raised student consciousness, but have had little success in prompting actual political work by students outside of school. In this chapter I extend the paradigm of our dominant type of neo-Marxist practice (classroom critical pedagogy) to suggest student activity in the political realm—crafting experiences for students in mounting or joining issue campaigns and public contestation in communities, district and corporate boardrooms, legislatures, and occasionally even the streets.

The first task of this chapter, though, is to update Marxist economic theory.

Accumulation by Dispossession

Marx described the closing of the feudal commons, wherein the British monarch gave land used jointly by peasants and aristocrats to aristocrats so they could graze sheep and sell the wool in emerging markets. The peasants were pushed off lands by their 'enclosure.' Marx called this process of privatizing public land 'primitive accumulation,' because it was a type of accumulation that preceded by centuries the more advanced means of making profit through industrial factory production. In 2005, Marxist geographer David Harvey theorized how Marx's identification of primitive accumulation can be appropriated today. It seems to me, and I hope to demonstrate below, that Harvey's appropriation and extension of Marx's theory increases the applicability of Marx to problems we face in both the economy and education.

In an advanced capitalist system such as our own, profits continue to be made by producing products and services sold to consumers and other businesses; but profits are increasingly accrued through the privatization of public resources. Public resources are 'capitalized'—they become sources of profit to their new private owners. People with great wealth in, say, hedge funds—most of which require a $500,000 to $1,000,000 investment to join—buy properties that had been held in common by the public at large (a city's drinking water, a transportation system, public pensions, or district schools) and convert them into private profit-making ventures. The tax-paying public no longer owns the drinking water, the pension system, or the schools. Harvey coined the term 'accumulation by dispossession' to describe this modern process of dispossessing the public (or persons) of what they owned, and turning it into private profit that can be accumulated by a few wealthy investors. In this form of profit taking, not only does the working class lose, as in traditional profit making in factories; we all lose (are dispossessed of ownership of) what we held in common as public water, air, pensions, schools, etc.

Accumulation by dispossession occurs when wealthy investors and corporations have excesses of money on hand for investment and profit-making, but no business or country to invest in that they believe will produce significant profits via production or services (because of war, recession, etc.). So they invest their money in financial risk taking and in capitalizing public goods. Harvey labels the excesses of capital 'over accumulation.' The term also applies to excesses of labor, as the lack of investment in production and services cause layoffs and firings of workers and employees.

An article in the *New York Times* in June, 2010, gives the flavor of the over accumulation of capital. The headline reads: On Wall Street, So Much Cash, So Little Time. The article describes hedge funds and banks that specialize in corporate takeovers as holding $500 billion dollars, and—in large part because of the world-wide recession—have nowhere profitable to invest it:

> Only on Wall Street, in the rarefied realm of buyout moguls, could you actually have too much money. Private equity firms, where corporate takeovers are planned and plotted, today sit atop an estimated $500 billion. But the deal makers are desperate to find deals worth doing, and the clock is ticking. Private equity funds generally tie up investors' money for 10 years. But they typically must invest all the money within the first three to five years of the funds' life. For giant buyout funds raised in 2006 and 2007, at the height of the bubble, time is short. They must invest their money soon or return

it to clients—presumably along with some of the management fees the firms have already collected.

(Creswell, 7/23/10)

In contrast to investment in traditional production, privatization and accumulation by dispossession do not increase the assets in a society. When you privatize water or other public goods such as pensions, you don't actually increase the stock of water or money in the pensions.

In order to fully grasp why privatization and accumulation by dispossession have come to prominence as economic activities, we need to understand the financialization of the economy: financialization instigates and encourages both privatization and accumulation by dispossession.

Economic Financialization

On the evening of September 18, 2008, Federal Reserve Chairman Ben Bernanke and Secretary of the Treasury Henry Paulson addressed Congressional leaders, informing them, in the words of the Senate Banking Committee Chair, "We are literally days away from a complete meltdown of our financial system, with all the implications here at home and globally" (Herszenhorn, 9/19/08). Despite an emergency infusion of federal money following the crash, lending by banks and other institutions soon ceased, and the financial system of the United States ground to a halt. Because the credit system was frozen (with no one willing to lend money), many industries and businesses—which typically depend on loans and other forms of credit to operate—were forced to slow or stop production. In the last three months of 2008, over a million and a half jobs were lost—the largest quarterly loss as a percentage of employment since the first quarter of 1975. In David Harvey's parlance, over a million and a half people were dispossessed of their livelihood.

A 'run' on hedge funds and investment banks had devalued and depleted their assets and exposed a global web of interconnected debts. World wide, the financial holdings of businesses, towns, counties, school systems, urban transportation systems, and in the case of Iceland an entire country, had been lost. In the U.S., about $7 trillion of U.S. shareholders' wealth—the gains of the previous six years—was wiped out. In addition, homeowners lost seven trillion dollars (Krugman, 2009). These losses represent further dispossession of the funds of many, as the financial system imploded.

A mere eight weeks after the financial implosion, at least 25 states, facing deficits, had cut or proposed to cut K-12 and early education, and at least 30 states had implemented or proposed cuts to public colleges and universities, while 39 states had imposed or planned cuts that hurt "vulnerable residents" (Johnson, Olif, and Koulish, 1/29/09, 1). Since then, 46 states have done so (McNichol, Olif, and Johnson, 7/15/10). These cuts have dispossessed the public—and particularly its vulnerable populations—of needed services.

Most economists attribute these losses to large, untenable risks taken by investors in an extremely financialized economy. Nobel laureate Paul Krugman (2009), for example, faults the extensive financialization of what he calls an unregulated "shadow banking system" (177). This unregulated shadow banking system expanded to rival or even surpass conventional banking in importance, and included hedge funds, banks, private equity funds, mortgage entities, and complicated speculative devices like Credit Default Swaps.

In a financialized economy, corporate profits that hitherto were invested in the 'real' economy (for production and the provision of services) are used for speculation in stock, mortgage, currency, and other markets. Investment in industry and services (e.g., in teachers, school buildings, factory expansion, or interstate highways) provides more widespread economic activity (i.e., stimulus) than money spent on speculation, whose activity and profits remain within the relatively small group of investors. Financial speculation propels income upwards, to the relatively small handful of investors with sufficient wealth to invest in, and therefore profit from, the private equity markets.

A primary method by which economic transactions are financialized is through securitization of debt and debt payment flows—the transformation of various types of financial assets and debts that are not convertible to cash into instruments that can be sold at a profit, or used to make speculative bets on the direction of asset prices of stocks, interest rates, currency levels, the price of oil or gas, etc. A prime example in the recent crisis is the securitization of home mortgages, which proceeds as follows. A bank or other mortgage issuing institution lends money to a home buyer in the form of a mortgage. Then, the bank sells the debt to a hedge fund or other entity that combines the mortgage with thousands of others. These bundles of mortgages are called 'securities.' Other investors then purchase the right to part of the income flow that results from the bundle as people pay their monthly mortgage fees. Before the investment bank sells this right to the income flow, it divides the pool of mortgages into many slices or 'tranches' (French for 'slice'). Each tranch can be bought and sold separately; the price of each slice is based on assumptions about the risk of the monthly payments—the riskier those payments are perceived to be, the lower the price anyone will pay for a slice of them, but the higher the interest will be. The sale of securities like bundled mortgages moves the risk of non-payment from the original bank or mortgage issuer to the buyer of the tranches—which means that the original lender is not concerned about the ability of the home buyer to pay his or her loan. This risk has been passed on to the hedge fund or other investor who typically passes it on to others as they purchase rights to part of the mortgage payment flows.

Over the last two decades, as the U.S. economy became less and less regulated, it became increasingly financialized. As a result of federal deregulation, by 2006 only about a quarter of all lending occurred in regulated sectors of the economy, down from about 80 percent 20 years before. Increasingly, profits of U.S. companies have derived from financial speculation rather than production. In the 1960s, profits from finance were 15 percent of all profits of all companies in the US; in 2006, almost half (40 percent) of all profits of U.S. companies came from finance—"a remarkable indication of the growth of financialization in the U.S. political economy" (Tabb, 2008, 5). The 10,000 hedge funds operating in 2007, before the crash, for example, constituted a huge part of the unregulated financialization system, and "accounted for half of all trading on the New York and London stock exchanges" in that year (ibid.).

Part of this increase in profits from speculation has occurred because non-financial companies have also increasingly accumulated profits through finance. By 2000, half (49.7 percent) of the profits of non-financial firms like General Motors (GM) and General Electric were from finance, not production. For some of the major non-financial companies—GM being a good example—the majority of their profits have come not from making products such as automobiles, but from their financial investment activities. In 2004, for example, GM lost money on cars, but made $2.9 billion on its financial activities. Indeed, by 2004, 'financial services'—a category comprised of finance, insurance, and real estate—far exceeded other sectors of the economy in size, totaling over one fifth of GDP—larger than manufacturing (at 12 percent) or health care, or wholesale/retail.

A good deal of the money for international speculation by U.S. investors has come from the privatization of publicly owned industries and companies here and in other nations. Little has been written about this aspect of privatization, although we have heard a great deal about privatization in the United States in regard to efforts by former President Bush to privatize social security, and current efforts via the promulgation of charter schools promoted by Race to the Top. But privatization, particularly during the 1980s and '90s, of public companies abroad provided huge investment and speculative opportunities for U.S. investors. For example, between 1984 and 1988, when Russia privatized and sold off its publicly owned oil fields and 225,000 of its publicly owned state companies, *The Wall Street Journal* inquired, "Looking for an investment that could gain 2,000 percent in three years? Only one stock market offers that hope …Russia" (Browning, 3/4/95). Journalist Naomi Klein reports that "many investment banks, including Credit Suisse First Boston, as well as a few deep-pocketed financiers, quickly set up dedicated Russian mutual funds" (2007, 231). And the Asian Crisis of 1997–98 also set off a wave of privatization, and U.S. and other multinationals invested heavily. Bechtel bought the water and sewage systems in Manila. "The New York-based energy giant Sithe got a large stake in Thailand's public gas company, …and Indonesia's water systems were split between Britain's Thames Water and France's Lyonnaise des Eaux" (ibid, 276). Privatization of public resources, the use of this money for international speculation, and the complex global interconnectedness of the deals were important causes of the turmoil in global markets that occurred in late 2008.

Because investment funds have gone primarily to speculation (rather than to investment in U.S. industry, public services, or infrastructure), the latter three have weakened. In regard to infrastructure, for example, bridges, public toll roads, transit equipment, electric power plants, and sewer systems are in disrepair nation wide, and to make up for disappearing state taxes (as businesses lose business, and fewer taxes are paid), some states and local governments put the public properties up for sale, sold them to hedge funds or banks, or leased them in quasi-privatization speculative deals called SILO/LILOs (Morcroft, 5/19/08; Morganson, 12/1/08). This puts the governments in a dangerous situation because when the deals collapse, the public authorities are placed in dire financial straights.

School districts, as well, have been caught up in the financial turmoil, and have been dispossessed of money they invested with wealthy hedge funds and banks. Chicago, Denver, Los Angeles, Philadelphia (and other districts in Pennsylvania), among other public entities like towns and cities, have lost almost 30 billion dollars in the last two years, as they have attempted to extract themselves from complicated financial arrangements that hedge funds and banks claimed would save them money (Morganson, 8/5/10).

Financial profits like those that result from financial deals made with public entities like districts, towns, and cities, are taxed at an extremely low rate of 15 percent, because they are counted by the Internal Revenue System as capital gains rather than income. Thus, taxes from almost all of the money used to gamble with is lost to the public purse. It was not always this way; in the post World War II decades, until John F. Kennedy's administration, high marginal tax rates (of up to 91 percent) on wealth took tax money and invested it in the public sphere.

As part of the public sphere, education districts in a financialized economy—especially in poor areas—are placed in danger, as state taxes disappear and deficits mount at the same time that state legislatures have taken over legal responsibility for the major portion of funding for school districts. The school districts become more vulnerable to privatization.

Neoliberalism

Accumulation by dispossession and financialization of the economy are processes that have become central to the economy largely as a result of neoliberalism, the political philosophy that some call 'market rule.' Neoliberal philosophy encouraged the deregulation of banks and other corporations, and the withdrawal of the state from many areas of social provision (such as welfare and other aspects of the social safety net that characterized economic policy making in the three decades after World War II). Neoliberalism had been promoted by conservative economists like Milton Friedman at the University of Chicago for decades before its adoption by the federal government. In the 1970s, Friedman's ideas were brought to center stage of policy making following Reagan's election in 1981. In the ensuing decades, Republican and Democratic Presidents and legislatures alike subscribed to neoliberal goals (Democrat Bill Clinton, for example, ended entitlement to welfare, and continued the deregulation of large banks). One of the key moments in the rise of neoliberalism was the debt crisis that occurred in the city of New York in the 1970s. In response to the urban crisis of the 1960s (widespread rebellions or 'riots' by African Americans in cities, for example), the federal government poured funds into inner cities to deal with race problems and unemployment, and the need for social services. City governments spent these funds on income support, the expansion of education, and the creation of public sector jobs for working-class New Yorkers. One result of this process was the increased strength of the unions and steep rises in public sector employment.

But as Ronald Reagan and the neoliberal philosophy took hold, federal government funding dried up. Money to inner cities was cut off, and city governments could either shed a large number of workers or they could borrow from the banks. They turned to the bankers. In an interview, David Harvey explains what happened in New York City.

> This borrowing [from the banks] was based partly on a boom in real estate in the early 1970s, which the city's administration was heavily involved in. When this market crashed in 1973 the city found itself vulnerable to the bankers. The bankers saw this as a possibility for them to launch a coup against the city—reshaping it according to a very different model [lower wages, weaker unions, and cuts in social services]. It's a bit like the Iraq war. They had wanted to go into Iraq in the early 1990s, but they couldn't do it. Then 9/11 gave them the opportunity they needed. In New York in the 1970s, the bankers lent money to the city and implemented a pioneering 'structural

adjustment programme,' shearing off a lot of public services and renegotiating labor contracts. It was a full frontal attack on the population of the city. Then of course they had to reconstruct it, because they had tremendous interests in real estate values, especially in Manhattan. This is when they started using public [resources] to rebuild the city around their project.

(Interview with Joseph Choonara, Feb. 2006, Socialist Review)

Harvey argues that neoliberalism and 'market rule' have fostered a major shift in class power to the benefit of a tiny elite. We see the consequence of this in the stark, unequal imbalances in U.S. society already discussed.

As journalist Naomi Klein (2007) has demonstrated, this tactic of seizing opportunities created by economic crisis to drive through free market policies (with privatization, wage suppression, service cuts, and therefore accumulation by dispossession at the center) has formed a pattern of political and economic elite activity ever since. The same investment bankers involved in the New York City crisis of the early 1970s, for instance, were involved in the debt crisis that hit Latin America in the 1980s. This time, though, they needed the federal government's power and money. The U.S. government, now led by Ronald Reagan, found a use for the International Monetary Fund (IMF), which many neoliberals had previously been suspicious of. Along with the World Bank, the IMF forced through neoliberal structural adjustment programs across Latin America in exchange for debt relief.

What does the addition of 'accumulation by dispossession' to the Marxist theoretical arsenal accomplish? I have been suggesting that this concept yields insights into our economy and resulting dangers from increased financialization and privatization. But I also believe that the concept provides a tool of defense against such theft. Accumulation by dispossession suggests a new orientation to fighting injustice. In addition to organizing at the 'point of production' in factories and offices, as Marxist theory has long prescribed by its focus on exploitation in workplaces, the prevalence of accumulation by dispossession suggests we need to organize society-wide. The struggle is no longer only of low-income, minority and white working-class families against the capitalist class. Working for progressive change now also involves all of us against the few political and economic elites who remove from our domain what has been rightfully ours: our jobs, income, homes, schools, water, pension funds, transportation systems, etc.

An important goal of this new orientation is to halt the theft of public goods by a small elite of investors. While traditional organizing of people at their work sites remains important, organizing in communities and schools increases in importance. And thus critical pedagogy becomes even more crucial to our efforts.

Extending Critical Pedagogy

This section of Chapter Four argues that in addition to extending Marxist theory, new conditions require an extension of our practice. Critical pedagogy is an enduring, important form of neo-Marxist practice for educators at all levels. In order to make this practice more effective in encouraging political participation by young people in struggles for social justice, we need to move our work beyond classroom walls into the worlds in which low-income, black and Latino, and immigrant students live. We can, in other words, involve our students in contestation in public places—public struggles over rights, injustice, and opportunity.

There are many reasons people get involved in political contestation, and having their consciousness raised (by, say, a teacher or friend) is a necessary, but not sufficient, cause of engagement. The processes that research suggests are most important in encouraging a person's involvement in political contestation are discussed below. I describe each mechanism, offer an example from history—typically from the U.S. Civil Rights Movement, because of my personal involvement in that struggle, and my research on the Movement for *Radical Possibilities*—and then relate my point to the work of critical pedagogy. The first two processes may be common to much critical teaching, but the rest are not, and can provide a crucial direction for future activity.

The first process influencing whether people become involved in political contention has to do with how they interpret their political and economic surroundings—and changes in those. To be willing to engage in social protest, people must view current developments as presenting opportunities for waging struggle. As I point out in previous chapters, the deterioration of wage and job opportunities, and the diminishing rewards for college completion by low-income students, all need to be seen as openings through which to push for equity. This apprehension of new opportunities sometimes helps us to see old arrangements in a new light. Situations that were previously understood as oppressive but immutable can be reimagined and viewed as useful.

An historical example of this process of attribution of opportunity can be seen in the 1930s and 1940s, when black

Americans were becoming consumers in the economies of Southern and Northern cities. Many realized they had new leverage over businesses where they shopped. 'Don't buy where you can't work' campaigns of the 1930s, and sit ins and boycotts of restaurants and other pubic facilities by black college students in the 1940s, as well as 1947 Freedom Rides to test interstate bus segregation—all took advantage of the economic changes affecting African Americans, interpreting them as an opportunity for gaining rights. Critical educators today have an important role to play in helping students apprehend possibility in what, at first glance, might appear overdetermined or unchangeable racial, class, or gender subordination.

Closely related to attribution of opportunity is the process whereby people appropriate existing organizations and institutions to make them more radical, to change their function, purpose, or manner of operating, so that they are more useful for transgressive politics.

The Southern black church during the 1950s and 1960s is a salient instance of this process. Until the 1950s, most black church leaders in the South saw their churches as preparation for personal salvation, not as a way to change the present. In the 1950s, many congregants and pastors appropriated the church and transformed it into a major tool of the civil rights struggle. The extensive committee structure and community activities of women members were appropriated for civil rights; the format and activities of the Sunday service were altered somewhat to provide the structure and tone of mass political meetings; extensive, widespread church networks among pastors were energized and organized for planning and sharing protest information. These institutions were already part of the black experience. Only minor, but crucial, alterations in form, purpose, or mode of functioning needed to be made to encourage people to participate in protest.

Critical educators are involved in a similar, vital process of reimagining schools and classrooms as social justice building spaces. This work is incredibly difficult but, I would argue, not any more impossible than the reimagining of economic relations, the church, and culture that black Americans undertook to achieve the victories of the civil rights movement.

Reimagining economic change and institutions as potentially oppositional does not, by itself, bring social change. And developing critical consciousness in people through information, readings, and discussion does not, by itself, induce them to participate in transgressive politics—although it provides a crucial base of understanding. To activate people to create or join public contention, it is important to actually involve them in protest activity of some kind (McAdam, Tarrow, and Tilly, 2001; Payne, 1995).

To make the point that involvement in protest is necessary to further involvement, sociologists studying the civil rights movement argue that people do not "become political" and then take part in contention; rather, participation in contention creates new, politicized identities: "identities modify in the course of social interaction" (McAdam, Tarrow, and Tilly, 2001, 126; see also studies in psychology and anthropology gathered by Dorothy Holland, 2001).

In other words, shifts in political identity do not so much motivate contentious political action, as develop as a logical consequence of it. One develops a political identity and commitment—a change in consciousness—from joining demonstrations, marching, singing, joining the activities of social justice organizations in one's neighborhood, etc. Participation creates individual participants; and it also leads to groups developing their own collective identity as social change agents.

As Southern sharecroppers began to register to vote, and continued in this personally dangerous, politically contentious activity, a new collective identity was constructed by them individually and as a group. They came to see themselves, and they became—individually and as a 'class'—a new category: Black citizens who were entitled to representation, entitled to their 'rights.' Such 'signifying work' was evident at the close of the successful Montgomery Bus Boycott in 1956. As Dr. Martin Luther King noted, the courageous, organized, successful actions of the participants in the boycott "had rendered the conventional identities—members of this or that congregation [or] 'our Negroes' for example—inadequate descriptors of the celebrants." After the boycott, King described the 'new Negro': "[W]e walk in a new way. We hold our heads in a new way." The boycott not only changed the laws in Montgomery, but helped to create, and became an expression of, "a new collective identity among Southern blacks generally"—a result of participation (ibid., 319, 301).

In order to develop a sense of themselves as change agents, as active political players, youth also need opportunities to engage in such activity. The suggestions at the close of Chapter Two provide examples for extending critical teaching into communities and other arenas. I am aware of three additional books that powerfully describe the engagement of teachers and students in political contestation: *Beyond Resistance! Youth Activism and Social Change* (Noguera, et al, 2006); *Black*

Youth Rising: Activism and Radical Healing in Urban American (Ginwright, 2009); and *Revolutionizing Education:Youth Participatory Action Research* (Camorata and Fine, 2008).

Engagement itself, then, is a necessary part of taking up further engagement. Like riding a bike, one has to do it to learn to do it.

There is an additional, very important reason that people become active, and that is that they are part of organizations or networks that are already active.

Sociologist Doug McAdam analyzed the applications of northern college students who applied to be part of the civil rights movement's Freedom Summer of registering black voters in 1964 Mississippi. He found that of 1,000 applicants accepted into the program, those who came South to participate (as opposed to those who were accepted but did not come) had "much stronger links to the Summer Project than did the no-shows. They were more likely to be members of civil rights or allied groups, have friends involved in the movement, and have more extensive histories of civil rights activity prior to the summer…in fact nothing distinguish[ed] the two groups more clearly than this contrast [in] social proximity to the project" (1988, 65).

McAdam's analysis suggests that belonging to a social group or network increases a person's chances of participation in contentious politics; and in this phenomenon we also find important evidence that initial participation makes further participation more likely.

For participation, available organizations are joined; the networks of people connected to an organization are made known; and being part of these is critical. A crucial consequence of being part of such embeddedness is that one is more likely to be asked to join contention; being asked to join has been found to be one of the best predictors of participation.

When educators plan for student participation in pedagogy involving organizing an issue campaign in the local community, in conjunction with others already so engaged (as described in Chapter Two), they are in effect asking (recruiting) their students into networks, and engaging them in an activity through which they are likely to be asked to participate further.

A sense of efficacy—achieved through actual participation—is also among the strongest predictors of subsequent participation. When critical educators involve students in contention via issue campaigns, we teach students the civic skills necessary for meaningful participation. We provide opportunities for them to develop the skills and experience, the successes, which can create in them a sense of efficacy as change agents and effective actors in their communities.

Indeed, research has substantiated these as benefits that accrue to youth who work to further opportunity in their communities. Studies have documented that such civic activism by low-income students of color, for example, typically fosters their positive personal development, and improves their academic engagement and, therefore, achievement (see, for example, Benson and Leffert, 1988; Forum for Youth Investment, 2004; Roth and Brooks-Gunn, 1998; Zeldin and Price, 1995). Thus, research demonstrates that organizing urban youth to work with others to improve their schools and neighborhoods gives teenagers connections, embedding them in constructive community networks. This connectedness is a worthy alternative to that offered by most street gangs.

In addition, by organizing others to work responsibly for social change, minority youth counter the dominant society's view that they are a social problem. Teens also are encouraged to understand how the poverty of their families and their peers may arise from systemic rather than personal failings. And it provides them with the concrete lesson that they can bring about changes in society, giving them a foundation for pursuing this kind of activity as adults.

I have been discussing evidence that although critical educators do well to share with students information about systemic causes of subordination, that is not enough to get students involved in the struggle for social justice. There are important lessons to take from this discussion, including the need to assist students in interpreting economic and political developments as opportunities for participation, helping them to appropriate existing institutional and organization forms for providing physical and emotional support for—and curriculum that engages students directly in—actual public contention and the development of themselves as active agents in their own and their communities' futures. When educators in the mid-20th century added 'student council,' voting, and school wide elections to American high schools, they might have been acting on this same principle. The early educators must have assumed that participation in the processes of democracy would legitimate these in the eyes of the students. And, most likely, they hoped that participation in the processes of democracy while in high school would encourage further participation later on. Critical pedagogy today ought to be based on the same principle. By giving students direct experience with social justice work, we can educate them to appreciate and value those forms of democratic process that are aimed specifically at creating a more equitable society—-public contention toward progressive social change. By setting up situations in the school experience that allow practice of, and assisting students to acquire skill with, public political contention, we legitimize this work and develop students' predisposition to engage in it.

Reading the *New York Times* on July 23, 2010

Every morning I read the *New York Times* on the computer, as I sip my morning coffee. On July 23, the day that I would complete a solid draft of the last chapter of this book, four stories caught my eye:

> Ford's Rebound Rolls on as It Posts $2.6 Billion Profit. This article praises Ford Motor Company for recovering from the recession. "In two years, the Ford Motor Company has gone from losing the most money in its history to earning $26 million a day in the second quarter of 2010."
>
> (Bunkley, 7/23/10)

> Federal Report Faults Banks on Huge Bonuses. In this report we learn that with the financial system in collapse in 2008, "a group of troubled banks doled out more than $2 billion in bonuses and other payments to their highest earners." The Obama administration "is expected to name 17 financial companies that made questionable payouts totaling $1.58 billion immediately after accepting billions of dollars of taxpayer aid…"
>
> (Dash, 7/23/10)

> Economic Insecurity: The Long View. Reporting on a new study by the Rockefeller Foundation, this story relates that "in the last decade

… one in five Americans … has experienced a decline of 25 percent or more in available household income. The typical American experiencing such a plunge will require six to eight years just to climb back to previous levels of income."

(Powell, 7/23/10)

Once a Leader, U.S. Lags in College Degrees. This article tells us that "the College Board warned Thursday that the growing gap between the United States and other countries [in college attainment] threatens to undermine American economic competitiveness. "The United States used to lead the world in the number of 25- to 34-year-olds with college degrees. Now it ranks 12th among 36 developed nations. … Canada is first …"

(Lewin, 7/23/10)

These four stories seemed to confirm in one day's news much of what I had written in this book. We hear that one of the largest corporations is making billions in profit, although the country is in recession and many millions are out of work or are underemployed. We learn that some of the billions of taxpayer dollars we spent to save the largest banks were used for bonuses to those who were instrumental in causing the financial implosion that rocked the economy and caused the unemployment and joblessness. And research by a major foundation reveals that the average person in the U.S. has been dispossessed of six to seven years worth of income because of the crash. In the last story we see that education is called upon to solve our economic problems (in this case, economic competitiveness).

As I read the *New York Times* that day, I didn't know whether to laugh or cry. Do I feel joy because my arguments in this book had been affirmed by the daily news, or do I feel despair because what they wrote, and what I have written, is devastating in its implications? Perhaps the most appropriate response came later: anger and determination—anger at what is unfair, and determination to work harder to make things right.

Perhaps all these emotions are called for. Yet importantly, I want to end this book with positive feelings of gratitude and hope. I am thankful to all the colleagues who over the years have taken the road less traveled, and gone to Marx for inspiration. Marx has been much maligned, and is in need of proper reconsideration. My hope is that this volume will contribute to his restitution, and to his utility as a theoretical and practical tool for educators.

REFERENCES

Advisory Committee on Student Financial Assistance. (2010). *The rising price of inequality*. Washington, DC: www.ed.gov/acsfa.

Anyon, Jean. (1980). Social class and the hidden curriculum of work. *Journal of Education*, 162(1), 7–42.

Anyon, Jean. (1981). Social class and school knowledge. *Curriculum Inquiry*, 11(1), 3–42.

Anyon, Jean. (1983). Toward useful theory. *Theory into Practice*, 21 (1), 1982: 34–38.

Anyon, Jean. (1984). Intersections of gender and class: Accommodation and resistance by working-class and affluent females to contradictory sex-role ideologies. *Journal of Education*, 166(1), 25–48.

Anyon, Jean. (1993). The retreat of Marxism and socialist feminism: Postmodern and poststructural theories in education. *Curriculum Inquiry*, 24(2), 115–134.

Anyon, Jean. (1994). Teacher development and reform in an inner city school. *Teachers College Record*, 96(1), 14–31.

Anyon, Jean. (1995a). Race, social class, and educational reform in an inner city school. *Teachers College Record*, 97(1), 69–94.

Anyon, Jean. (1995b). Inner city school reform: Toward useful theory. *Urban Education*, 30(1), 56–70.

Anyon, Jean. (1997). *Ghetto schooling: A political economy of urban educational reform*. New York: Teachers College Press.

Anyon, Jean. (2005). *Radical possibilities: Public policy, urban education, and a new social movement*. New York and London: Routledge.

Anyon, Jean. (2006).What counts as educational policy: Notes toward a new paradigm. *Harvard Educational Review*, 75(1), 65–88.

Anyon, Jean. (2009). *Theory and educational research: Toward critical social explanation*. New York and London: Routledge.

Anyon Jean, and Kiersten Greene. (2007). No Child Left Behind as an anti-poverty measure. *Teacher Education Quarterly*, (34)2, 157–162.

Apple, Michael. (1979). *Ideology and curriculum*. New York and London: Routledge.

Apple, Michael. (1993). *Official knowledge: Democratic curriculum in a conservative age*. New York and London: Routledge.

Apple, Michael. (1996). *Cultural politics and education*. New York and London: Routledge.

Apple, Michael. (2001). *Educating the 'right' way: Markets, standards, God, and inequality*. New York and London: Routledge.

Benson, Peter, and Nancy Leffert. (1988). Beyond the 'village' rhetoric: Creating healthy communities for children and adolescents. *Journal of Applied Developmental Studies*, 2,135–158.

Bourdieu, Pierre. (1973). Cultural reproduction and social reproduction. In *The structure of schooling: Readings in the sociology of education*. Richard Arum and Irenee Beattie, Editors. New York: McGraw Hill: 56–68.

Bowen, William, Mathew Chingos, and Michael McPherson. (2009). *Crossing the finish line: Completing college at America's public universities*. Princeton, NJ: Princeton University Press.

Bowles, Samuel and Herbert Gintis. (1976). *Schooling in capitalist America*. New York: Basic Books.

Bracey, Gerald. (2005). *No Child Left Behind: Where does the money go?* Policy Brief, Education Policy Studies Laboratory. Education Policy Research Unit. Arizona State University.

Browning, Jim. (March 24, 1995). Bond investors gamble on Russian stocks. *Wall Street Journal*.

Bunkley, Nick. (July 23, 2010). Ford's rebound rolls on as it posts $2.6 billion profit. *New York Times*.

Burch, Patricia. (2009). *Hidden markets: The new educational privatization*. New York and London: Routledge.

Camorata, Julio, and Michelle Fine, editors. (2008). *Revolutionizing education: Youth participatory action research*. New York and London: Routledge.

Carnevale, Anthony and Jeff Strohl. (2010). How increasing college access is increasing inequality, and what to do about it. In *Rewarding strivers: Helping low-income students succeed in college. Richard Kahlenberg, editor. New York: Century Foundation Press, 71–190.

Center for Youth Development and Policy Research. (2010). National Community Youth Mapping site. www.communityyouthmapping.org.

Choonara, Joseph. (April, 2009). Interview with David Harvey. Socialist Review. http://www.socialistreview.org.uk/article.php?article number=10801.

Creswell, Julie. (July 23, 2010). On Wall St., so much cash, so little time. New York Times.

Darder, Antonia. (1991). Culture and power in the classroom. Westport, Connecticut: Bergin and Garvey.

Dash, Eric. (July 23, 2010). Federal report faults banks on big bonuses. New York Times.

Emery, Kathy. (2002). The Business Roundtable and systemic reform. Unpublished dissertation, University of California Davis.

Emery, Kathy. (2007). Corporate control of public schools. Teacher Education Quarterly, 34(2), 25–44.

Engels, Friedrich. (1882/1989). Letter to Eduard Bernstein. Marx and Engels, Collected Works. 46, 353. New York: International Publishers.

Filion, Kay. (2009). Minimum wage issue guide. Economic Policy Institute. Washington, DC: Economic Policy Institute.

Fine, Michelle. (1991). Framing dropouts: Notes on the politics of an urban public high school. Albany, NY: SUNY Press.

The Forum for Youth Investment. (2004). From youth activities to youth action, 2(2).

Ginwright, Shawn. (2009). Black youth rising: Activism and radical healing in urban America. New York: Teachers College Press.

Giroux, Henry. (1983). Theory and resistance in education. Santa Barbara, CA: Praeger.

Harvey, David. (2005). The new imperialism. New York and London: Oxford University Press.

Harvey, David. (2007). A brief history of neoliberalism. New York and London: Oxford University Press.

Herszenhorn, David. (September,19, 2008). Congressional leaders stunned by warnings. New York Times.

Hoare, Quintin, and Geoffrey Nowell-Smith. (1971). Antonio Gramsci: Selections from the prison notebooks. Translated and edited by Quintin Hoare and Geoffrey Nowell-Smith. New York: International Publishers.

Holland, Dorothy. (2001). Identity and agency in cultural worlds. Cambridge, MA: Harvard University Press.

Johnson, Nicholas. Phil Olif, and Koulish (January 29, 2009). *Facing deficits, at least 39 states are imposing or planning cuts that hurt vulnerable residents*. Washington, DC: Center on Budget and Policy Priorities.

Kahlenberg, Richard, Editor. (2010). *Rewarding strivers: Helping low-income students succeed in college*. New York: Century Foundation Books.

Klein, Naomi. (2007). *The shock doctrine: The rise of disaster capitalism*. New York: Picador Press/Macmillan.

Krugman, Paul. (2009). *The return of depression economics and the crisis of 2008*. New York: W.W. Norton.

Lafer, Gordon. (2002). *The job training charade*. Ithaca, NY: Cornell University Press.

Lewin, Tamar. (July 23, 2010). Once a leader, U.S. lags in college degrees. *New York Times*.

Lipman, Pauline. (1998). *Race, class, and power in school restructuring*. Albany, NY: SUNY Press.

Lipman, Pauline. (2003). *High stakes education: Inequality, globalization, and urban school reform*. New York and London: Routledge.

Lipman, Pauline. (In press). *The new political economy of urban education: Neoliberal urbanism, race, and the right to the city*. New York and London: Routledge.

Marx, Karl. The Eighteenth Brumaire of Louis Bonaparte. (1852/1978). In *The Marx-Engels reader*, second edition. Edited by Robert Tucker. New York: W.W. Norton: 594–618.

Marx, Karl. (1859/1983). Preface to the Critique of Political economy. In *The portable Karl Marx*. Edited by Eugene Kamenka. New York: Penguin: 158–162.

Marx, Karl. (1869). International Workingmen's Association 1869. Record of Speeches by Karl Marx. First published in full in *Marx and Engels, Works*, 2nd Russian Edition, 1960. www.marxists.org/archive/marx/.../1869/education-speech.htm

Marx, Karl and Friedrich Engels. (1845/1998). The German ideology. In *The German ideology, including theses on Feuerbach*. Amherst, NY: Prometheus Books.

Marx, Karl and Friedrich Engels. (1848/2008). *The Communist manifesto*. New York and London: Oxford University Press.

McAdam, Doug. (1988) *Freedom summer*. New York: Oxford University Press.

McAdam, Doug, Sidney Tarrow, and Charles Tilly. (2001). *Dynamics of contention*. New York: Cambridge University Press.

McCarthy, Cameron. (1999). Reading the American popular: Suburban resentment and the representation of the inner city in contemporary film and T.V. *Race, Gender & Class*, 6 (2), 171–189.

McLaren, Peter. (2000). *Che Guevara, Paulo Freire, and the pedagogy of revolution*. Lanham, MD: Roman and Littlefield.

McNichol, Elizabeth, Phil Olif, and Nicholas Johnson. (July 15, 2010). *Recession continues to batter state budgets*. Washington, DC: Center on Budget and Policy Priorities.

Mishel, Lawrence, Jared Bernstein and Heidi Shierholz. (2009). *The state of working America: 2008/2009*. Washington, DC: Economic Policy Institute.

Morcroft, Gregory. (May 19, 2008). Citi-run group wins Pa. turnpike lease. MarketWatch, *Wall Street Journal*.

Morganson, Gretchen. (December 1, 2008). Just call this deal Hoosier baroque. *New York Times*.

Morganson, Gretchen. (August 5, 2010). Exotic deals put Denver schools deeper in debt. *New York Times*.

Noguera, Pedro. (2003). *City schools and the American dream: Fulfilling the promise of public education*. New York: Teachers College Press.

Noguera, Pedro, Julio Camorata, and Shawn Ginwright, editors. (2006). *Beyond resistance! Youth activism and community change*. New York and London: Routledge.

O'Connor, James. (1973). *The fiscal crisis of the state*. New York: St. Martin's Press.

Ornstein, Allan. (2007). *Class counts: Education, inequality, and the shrinking middle class*. Lantham, MA: Rowman and Littlefield.

Payne, Charles. (1995). *I've got the light of freedom: The organizing tradition and the Mississippi freedom struggle*. Berkeley, CA: University of California Press.

Perry, Theresa. (2004). *Young, gifted and black: Promoting high achievement among African American students*. Boston: Beacon Press.

Powell, Michael. (July 23, 2010). Economic insecurity: The long view. *New York Times*.

Reich, Robert. (In press). *Aftershock: The next economy and America's future*. New York: Knopf.

Roth, Jodi, and Jeanne Brooks-Gunn. (1998). Promoting healthy adolescence: Synthesis of youth development program evaluations. *Journal of Research on Adolescence*, (8), 423–459).

Shiller, Robert. (August 1, 2010). Economic view: What would Roosevelt do? *New York Times*.

Shor, Ira. (1992). *Empowering education: Critical teaching for social change*. Chicago: University of Chicago Press.

Tabb, Bill. (2008). The centrality of finance. *Journal of World Systems Research*, (13), 1–11.

The White House. (2010). Race to the Top. *The White House*. http://www.whitehouse.gov/the-press-office/fact-sheet-race-top

Third Presidential Debate. (Oct. 13, 2004)

Torres, Carlos and Raymond Morrow. (1995). *Social theory and education: A critique of theories of social and cultural reproduction*. Albany, NY: SUNY Press.

Watkins, Bill. (2001). *The white architects of black education: Ideology and power in America*. New York: Teachers College Press.

Weiler, Kathleen. (1994). Freire and a feminist pedagogy of difference. *Harvard Educational Review*, 61(4), 449–474.

Weis, Lois. (1990). *Working class without work: High school students in a de-industrializing economy*. New York and London: Routledge.

Zeldin, Shepard, and Lauren Price. (1995). Creating supportive communities for adolescent development: Challenges to scholars. *Journal of Adolescent Research*, (10), 6–15.

INDEX